United States
Department of
Agriculture

Forest Service

Southern
Research Station

General Technical
Report SRS–133

Faces from the Past:
Profiles of Those Who Led
Restoration of the South's Forests

James P. Barnett

Author:

James P. Barnett, Emeritus Scientist, USDA Forest Service, Southern Research Station, Pineville, LA.

Cover:

The cover photo was taken at the Roberts plots near Urania, LA, in April 1940. These plots, established in 1913, were used to study the effects of prescribed burning on longleaf pine growth and development. From left: H.H. Chapman of Yale University; U.S. Forest Service scientists C. Allen Bickford, H.H. Muntz, G.W. Trayer, Clarence L. Forsling, Roy A. Chapman, T.R. Truax, John Curry and J.M. Hughes; and Lloyd Blackwell, who became the Head of Louisiana Tech University's Department of Forestry.

Photo credit:

Unless otherwise noted, the photographs were from collections of the U.S. Forest Service, the Louisiana Forestry Commission (now Louisiana Office of Forestry), and the Louisiana Forestry Association. These organizations have extensive photo collections and many of the early photographs were interchanged between organizations so that the identity of many of the original photographers has been lost. Professional photographers Elemore Morgan and Tommy Kohara took many of these photographs. Sources for others are identified with the photograph.

Disclaimer

The use of trade or firm names in this publication is for reader information and does not imply endorsement by the U.S. Department of Agriculture of any product or service.

Pesticide Precautionary Statement

This publication reports research involving pesticides. It does not contain recommendations for their use, nor does it imply that the uses discussed here have been registered. All uses of pesticides must be registered by appropriate State and Federal agencies before they can be recommended.

CAUTION: Pesticides can be injurious to humans, domestic animals, desirable plants, and fish or other wildlife—if they are not handled or applied properly. Use all pesticides selectively and carefully. Follow recommended practices for the disposal of surplus pesticides and pesticide containers.

January 2011

Southern Research Station
200 W.T. Weaver Blvd.
Asheville, NC 28804

FACES FROM THE PAST:

PROFILES OF THOSE WHO LED RESTORATION OF THE SOUTH'S FORESTS

JAMES P. BARNETT

Abstract—Early in the 20th century, the forests in the South were devastated by aggressive harvesting and many millions of acres of forest land needed reforestation. Foresighted individuals began a committed effort to restore this land to a productive condition. This effort required dedication, cooperation, and leadership. A small cadre of individuals led the restoration of the South's forests that became the basis of the South's economy. Many of these individuals are profiled in this document.

Keywords: History of forestry research, research scientists, restoration of southern forests, significance of forestry to the South, southern pines.

PREFACE

When Europeans arrived on the shores of America, they encountered extensive forests that provided both a needed resource and a hindrance to establishing farm land critical for their existence. The forests provided materials for export as well as to build homes and cities. Initially, this resource was used slowly, but as the population increased timber near bays and rivers was harvested and shipped widely to meet an array of timber related needs.

Clearing of forests for crop production occurred throughout the southeastern Coastal Plain and Piedmont from the colonial period until the beginning of the Civil War (Williams 1989). In Virginia alone, more than 25 million acres, nearly one-half of the total land area, had been cleared by 1860. Soil erosion became a major problem. Declining soil productivity caused large amounts of agricultural land to be abandoned throughout the South by the end of the Civil War (Fox and others 2007).

After the Civil War, the South's economy was in shambles and forested land was inexpensive. This provided an opportunity for northern industrialists to purchase timber and labor to operate sawmills. Although this massive harvest of the South's virgin forests resulted in deforestation throughout the region, it did provide the economic basis for recovery of the South.

The development of railroads throughout the country made a rapid movement of the population into the Great Plains and West feasible with a great need for building materials. Also, newly developed railroads and steam powered logging and milling equipment provided the technology to quickly harvest and mill tremendous quantities of timber. These efforts focused on the western portion of the Gulf Coastal Plain where virgin pine forests had remained largely untouched.

Wakeley (1954) stated that there were 13 million acres of forest land in need of planting. Later, Wahlenberg (1960) estimated that 29 million acres needing planting. These conditions resulted from abusive agricultural practices that degraded soil productivity, coupled with exploitative timber harvesting without provision for regeneration.

Deforestation has occurred frequently since the beginning of civilization. There are many examples of resulting devastations to the climate, loss of fuel for cooking, massive soil erosion, reductions in wildlife populations, and general decline of the economy of regions where forests were lost. Many European settlers who came to America did so because of problems caused by deforestation in their home countries, and major deforestation continues to occur in many developing nations even today.

How could the United States avoid most of the problems resulting from regional deforestation? The answer came from a coordinated effort to develop reforestation guidelines. Forward thinking individuals in the forest industry, Federal and State governments, private landowners, and university groups were determined to restore the devastated lands into productive forest systems.

In the early 1900s, forestry was in its infancy in the United States. The Biltmore Forest School near Asheville, NC, was created as the first forestry school in the United States. However, a number of university programs rapidly followed. Cornell, Yale, Minnesota, and Michigan universities were leaders in developing strong forestry programs. It is somewhat ironic that foresters from northern universities came to the South to lead restoration efforts that were needed because much of the forest devastation in the South was created by northern industrialists a few decades earlier.

The purpose of this publication is to recount the contributions of many of the early individuals who played an important role in the restoration of the South's forest ecosystems. Their dedication and ability were remarkable, and I hope that a focus on some of these pioneers can convey the nature and scope of their contributions to the South's recovery and current economy.

Some bias may be perceived because many of those selected for focus worked in the West Gulf Region. Two things contribute to this situation. When the U.S. Forest Service established the Southern Station in 1921, it was headquartered in New Orleans, LA. It was one of the earliest forestry organizations in the South and had research responsibilities for the Coastal Plain Region from eastern Texas to Georgia, South Carolina, and Florida. Hence, many of the early foresters in the South worked out of the New Orleans office.

Also, my 50-plus years of forestry experience was in this western portion of the South. My career overlapped many of these early forestry leaders—hence, I have more information about them. I hope that readers can gain an appreciation of the influence of these and other individuals who led the restoration of our South's forest resources.

I would like to express my sincere appreciation to a few individuals who helped insure the completion of this effort. Helen Derr, widow of Harold Derr who is profiled in the document, read it and made editorial corrections. Her career as a newspaper writer made this assistance invaluable. Paul Y. Burns, Ph.D., Emeritus Professor and retired head of Louisiana State University School of Forestry, Wildlife and Fisheries, provided encouragement, information on a number of those profiled, and editorial assistance. I also express my appreciation to my wife, Jena, who supported me in the effort.

James P. Barnett
Pineville, LA

TABLE OF CONTENTS

PREFACE iii

INTRODUCTION 1

  Naval Stores 2

  The Great Harvest of Pine Forests 3

  The South's Devastated Forests 4

  Growing Interest in Management and Reforestation 6

INDIVIDUALS WHO LED RESTORATION OF THE SOUTH'S FORESTS 7

  The Coming of Forestry to the South 7

    Father of Forestry in the South 7

      Henry E. Hardtner 7

    Early "Transient" Foresters in the South 9

      William W. Ashe 9

      Wilbur R. (Matty) Mattoon 10

      Austin Cary 10

    Reforestation Pioneer 11

      Philip C. (Phil) Wakeley 11

    Pioneer Nursery Specialist and Silviculturist Extraordinary 12

      F.O. (Red) Bateman 12

    The Nation's First Industrial Forester? 14

      J.T. (Jake) Johnson 14

    The First Forest Survey of the South 15

      Inman F. (Cap) Eldredge 15

      Philip R. (Phil) Wheeler 16

  Administration 17

    Great Southern Lumber Company 17

      William H. (Col. Bill) Sullivan 17

    Southern Forest Experiment Station 19

      Reginald D. (Reggie) Forbes 19

      Elwood L. (Demmie) Demmon 20

    Kisatchie National Forest's Longest Serving Supervisor 21

      Hugh S. Redding 21

    Legendary Ranger of Winn Ranger District 22

      George M. Tannehill, Jr. 22

    Louisiana Forestry Commission 23

      Victor Hugo Sonderegger 23

      James E. (Jim) Mixon 24

      Hans Enghardt 25

    Louisiana Forestry Association 27

      J.H. (Jim) Kitchens, Jr. 27

      Charles H. (Charlie) Lewis, Jr. 28

  Forest Management 29

    Uneven-aged Pine Management 29

      Russell R. (Russ) Reynolds 29

    Even-aged Pine Silviculture 30

      William F. (Bill) Mann, Jr. 30

    Direct Seeding 31

      Harold J. Derr 31

TABLE OF CONTENTS
(CONTINUED)

Statistics and Mensurational Techniques..33
    Roy A. Chapman..33
    Frank Freese..34
    Lewis R. (Lew) Grosenbaugh..34
Control of Upland Hardwoods...35
    Fred A. Peevy..35
Hardwood Management...37
    John A. (Put) Putnam..37
Forest Seed Production...38
    Howell C. Cobb...38
Consulting Forestry..39
    Leslie K. (Les) Pomeroy..39
    Zebulon W. (Zeb) White...40

Education...41
    Biltmore Forest School..41
        Carl A. Schenck...41
    Teacher, Artist, Conservationist, and "Mother of the Kisatchie National Forest".....42
        Caroline C. Dormon..42
    Yale University Forestry Training at Urania...43
        H.H. (Chappy) Chapman...43
    Louisiana State University School of Forestry..45
        Major J.G. Lee, Sr...45
        Ralph W. Hayes...46
        A. Bigler Crow...47
    Louisiana Tech University...47
        Lloyd P. (Black) Blackwell..47
    University of Arkansas at Monticello...48
        Henry H. (Hank) Chamberlin..48

Forest Products..49
    Mr. Pulp and Paper of the South..49
        Charles H. Herty...49
    Control of Blue-Stain Fungus...51
        Ralph M. (Lindy) Lindgren...51
    Timber Harvesting...51
        Albert E. (Wack) Wackerman...51
    Premier Wood Scientist..52
        Peter Koch...52

Forest Resources...53
    Soil Erosion and Flood Control..54
        H.G. (Mac) Meginnis..54
    Prescribed Fire..55
        H.H. (Chappy) Chapman...55
    Wildlife Conservation...56
        Bryant A. Bateman...56
        Claude H. (Grits) Gresham..57
    Forest Pathology...58
        George H. Hepting...58
    Tree Improvement and Genetics..59
        Philip C. (Phil) Wakeley...59
        Bruce J. Zobel...60

TABLE OF CONTENTS
(CONTINUED)

Photography/History 61
    Forestry Photography 62
        Tommy T. Kohara 62
        Elemore Morgan, Sr. 62
    Forestry History 63
        Edward F. (Ed) Kerr, Sr. 63
        Anna C. Burns 64

CONCLUSIONS 66

ACKNOWLEDGMENTS 67

LITERATURE CITED 68

INTRODUCTION

For generations the South has been thought of as an agricultural land with cotton and other agricultural crops as the basis of the area's economy. Many have not realized that it is one of the great forested regions of the world. Six out of every 10 acres of its land area were, and still are, in forests.

The original forests of the South consisted of four general types. Extending throughout the Coastal Plain were pure stands of longleaf and slash pine. Further inland into the highlands were forests of loblolly and shortleaf pine, either pure or mixed with hardwoods. The mountainous areas were mixed forests of upland hardwoods. Bottomland hardwoods, the fourth type, stretched along the banks and flatlands adjacent to the numerous creeks and rivers. By area, pine and hardwood forests were approximately equal.

The southern pinery was awesome in its vastness. Interrupted by occasional bottomland swamps, the pine forests stretched throughout the Coastal Plain from Virginia to the Texas plains in what the early settlers must have considered an endless expanse—a distance of nearly 1,500 miles. The longleaf pine forests themselves were estimated at 90 million acres. It was inconceivable that this enormous supply of wood might someday be consumed and that there would be a landscape of devastated forests.

These forests were looked upon by early settlers as both a blessing and a curse. They provided the wood products needed to build homes, towns, and cities, but they were an obstacle in developing agricultural land for producing food crops. They did provide some of the earliest products that could be marketed to England and other countries. These forest products helped build an economy that sustained the colonies.

Longleaf pine forests extended along the lower coastal plain from Virginia to eastern Texas. They were maintained by repeated use of fire. The longleaf pine forests originally covered about 90 million acres.

NAVAL STORES

One of the earliest and most colorful industries in the United States was the naval stores industry. During colonial days, the British navy eagerly sought tar and pitch obtained in abundance from pines along the southern Atlantic coast. The name "naval stores" comes from the use of tree resin to treat the rigging and caulking of sailing ships. In the earliest methods, the resinous heart wood of pines, especially longleaf pine, was burned in shallow pits dug in the forest. The molten resin or tar was drained off for use. The term "tar heels" for North Carolinians comes from the early days when naval stores production was of major importance.

The naval stores industry was an important one. For more than a century, the United States was the world's largest producer of naval stores (Demmon 1937). The two basic products, rosin and turpentine, were either derived from the living tree, from distillation of virgin longleaf pine stumps,

or as a byproduct in the manufacture of Kraft paper. Tapping living trees was the technology that was used for many decades. Distillation of longleaf pine stumps was a method developed after most of the virgin longleaf forests were harvested. Currently, naval stores products are a byproduct of the Kraft paper making process.

Technology for collecting pine resin from living trees consisting of nailing cups and gutters to selected trees was developed in 1902 by Charles Herty (Reed 1995). The previous "box" system was a ruinous technique that resulted in tree mortality in a few years (Reed 1982). Gutters were metal strips which directed the gum from streak to cup. Each week from March through October a streak of one-half to three-quarters of an inch deep was cut, or "chipped," into the tree above the gutter by means of a sharp tool called a hack. By the end of the chipping season, the streaks formed a continuous face extending almost a half way round the tree and 18 to 24 inches high. After several seasons, a face might

Tapping longleaf and slash pines for resin was a common practice in the 19th century and early 20th century. Naval stores provided major economic products from southern forests.

A typical face worked for producing resin. Naval stores production was very labor intensive work.

THE GREAT HARVEST OF PINE FORESTS

With exception of areas accessible from rivers and bays in the Southeast, the harvest of the vast timberland of the South was slow until after the Civil War. Movement of timber was primarily by wagons and oxen—both slow and labor intensive. However, the situation changed rapidly in the late 1800s when the development of railroads improved access into the vast timbered lands.

Also, after the Civil War the South's economy was devastated and land was very inexpensive. Forests in the Northeast and Midwest were rapidly being depleted. Investors from the North saw opportunities in the South and bought huge acreages of forest land, built sawmills, and began to produce lumber products for the rapidly expanding needs of industrial development. The longleaf pine forests of the Coastal Plain provided excellent opportunities for such enterprises because resources and labor were readily available.

Facilitating the development of the lumbering enterprises was the development of railroad logging. Not only were steam-powered locomotives common, but steam-powered skidders and loaders were developed that made the harvest of timber very efficient. The expansion of such lumbering enterprises in the late 1800s and early 1900s began a period called the "golden years" of lumbering in the South. During this period, sawmills were common in most communities throughout the South and, in fact, many towns and cities were developed around lumbering companies. Almost any town would have

extend up the tree 8 feet or more. After a tree had two high faces, it was generally considered to be "worked out."

About once a month the gum, known as dip, was transferred from cup to dip bucket and then to dip barrel. Mule drawn wagons conveyed the barrels from the woods to a still where distillation of the crude gum yielded turpentine and rosin. The thousands of small crude stills, once such common landmarks throughout the coastal region of the South, were gradually replaced by a few dozen large centralized plants of modern design and operation. However, working the trees faces and collecting the gum was never mechanized and remained a very labor-intensive process. After World War II, the labor to work the tree faces gradually disappeared. The harvest of virgin longleaf pine stumps for naval stores products continued into the late 1960s when the supply of these was exhausted. Now, the Kraft paper making process supplies the chemical products that historically came directly from the trees.

Railroad logging had a great effect on the harvest of the old-growth pine stands. Logging by this method spread rapidly across the South in the late 1800s and early 1900s.

one or more sawmills that provided labor, income, and drove the recovery of the economy. Along major railroad lines, small mills were almost in sight of one another. One author wrote, "If one had forgotten to sound its daybreak whistle calling labors to work, the blasts from neighboring mill would stir the neighbors to wakefulness."

Many sawmills were relatively small, but some were huge. The Great Southern Lumber Company (Great Southern) completed its mill in Bogalusa, LA, in 1907. The Great Southern became the largest mill in the South with four 8-foot band saws which ran at full speed for more than two decades and produced more than one-million board feet of lumber every 24 hours. Typical of many mills, the Goodyear family of Pennsylvania established a town to support its mill. In 1906, the town consisted of a number of large buildings and more than 700 dwellings.

Not only did railroad logging provide rapid transport of timber from the woods, the tracks could be moved frequently to continually access more and more timber. Also, the advent of the steam-powered skidders and loaders that operated on the tracks made handling of logs efficient. One steam-powered skidder could harvest logs from a 40-acre tract without having to relocate. The cable systems powered by the skidders were so powerful that they destroyed any timber that was not merchantable (Clark 1984). So, much of the resulting cutover land was without any means of natural regeneration.

Clyde steam-powered skidders provided an efficient means of harvesting timber. However, they were extremely destructive knocking down any trees that were not cut.

By the end of the 1920s, many hundreds of sawmills had cut all their available timber and ceased operations. In their wake were left "ghost towns" or towns able to maintain only a feeble existence (Forbes 1923). Many of the larger companies moved their equipment to the remaining great body of virgin timber in the West. A greater number were liquidated. For all practical purposes, the old-growth pine forests had disappeared from the South. In the Capper Report of 1920, the U.S. Forest Service (Forest Service) made the statement that "in 15 years the South will become dependent for its own needs upon large importations of lumber from the Pacific Coast" (Heyward 1958).

THE SOUTH'S DEVASTATED FORESTS

As early as the late 1910s, millions of acres of cutover land spread across the South. Development of the lumbering industry brought jobs and businesses, but when the timber was cut out there was bleakness and a spirit of desolation. The magnitude of the cutover land problem was brought in focus when a survey was made by the Southern Pine Association in 1919. The cutover land equaled the combined areas of Alabama, Mississippi, and Louisiana. This survey reported that 92 million acres of land had most of the timber removed (Heyward 1958). Boyd (2001) quotes R.D. Forbes of stating in 1923 that "the plain truth of the matter is that in county after county, in State after State of the South, the piney woods are not passing but *have passed."* (Emphasis is Forbes'.)

Not all of this land was barren stump-land since all sawmills did practice the same degree of utilization, nor did all make use of steam skidders, a form of logging which caused great damage to any timber left standing. However, little of this acreage was capable of becoming productive again without help. Cutover lands were a man-made problem and required a man-made solution.

In 1917, a Cut-Over Land Conference of the South was held in New Orleans, LA. Of 340 people registered, only four were foresters. Most were representatives of railroads, lumbermen, and specialists in all lines of agriculture. Although timber growing was recommended by some as the solution of the cutover problem, the sentiment of the meeting was in favor of converting forest land for livestock grazing.

There was widespread condemnation of the lumbermen for stripping the land. In 1904, Gifford Pinchot of the Forest Service stated, "It is evident that never before has forest destruction been as rapid as at present, that we have never been so near to exhaustion of our lumber supply and that

vigorous measures have never been as urgently required as now" (Heyward 1958).

Although the lumbermen justly bore the brunt of much criticism, in some respects they were unable to change the direction of the destruction. First, in the beginning there was no intention of returning to the lands logged over. The trees were 150 to 250 years old. It was beyond human capacity to conceive of a means whereby private capital might restore timber whose age at maturity was reckoned, not in decades, but centuries.

Second, the logging methods used by the large mills in the early days precluded activities commonplace today. Interest rates and depreciation on equipment, especially railroads, made impossible the cutting of a portion of the timber from an area and returning for a second cut in later years. Therefore, all merchantable timber was harvested.

Finally, local tax structure was a perplexing problem confronting early sawmills. As timber was cut, the tax levy was increased on the remainder. This prompted the mills to even greater efforts to liquidate their timber. Situations such as these were widespread and were a factor responsible for the cutout and get-out policy (Chapman 1912).

This area became a part of the Palustris Experimental Forest and represented millions of acres of cutover forests across the South.

There were other reasons why lumbermen did not consider forestry. First, these individuals knew little or nothing of forestry. Even as late as 1925, there were only a few foresters practicing in the entire South. Second, one report cited another reason why private interests could not practice forestry. It stated, "so long as excellent tracts of fine, virgin yellow pine could be purchased from $3 to $6 per thousand feet, it was of course manifestly impossible for any individual to give serious consideration to the encouragement of second growth" (Heyward 1958).

GROWING INTEREST IN MANAGEMENT AND REFORESTATION

It is interesting to note that the first steps in private forestry in the South came from progressive men in the naval stores industry. They were among the first to undertake on a commercial scale the growing of new crops (Heyward 1958). They learned how to minimize damage from their intentional fires and developed prescribed burning to a considerable degree before the forestry profession as a whole would admit the practice was possible. Their efforts received little praise because no practice was more ruinous to a pine forest than a typical early-day naval stores operation.

As the 20th century began, the newly created Forest Service began receiving requests for advice on timber growing from lumber companies and individuals widely scattered about the South. To be able to respond to these requests, the Forest Service recruited a few individuals with forestry experience related to the issues of concern. Although they had little forestry training, these individuals had exceptional ability to observe nature, draw tentative conclusions, and make practical recommendations. The most notable of these were Austin Cary, W.W. Ashe, and W.T. Mattoon. They were headquartered in Washington, DC, but traveled widely throughout the South.

Also at the turn of the century, it was apparent that there was a critical need for forestry training and education. Gifford Pinchot, who became Chief of the Forest Service, had established a forestry program at George Vanderbilt's estate near Asheville, NC. After leaving the Biltmore Estate, he recommended that Carl A. Schenck, a professionally trained forester from Germany, be hired to establish a forestry school. The Biltmore Forest School was established in 1898 and its curriculum focused on providing practical forest management field training supplemented with traditional classroom lectures. Established universities such as Cornell, Minnesota, Michigan, and Yale each created forestry schools shortly after the Biltmore experiment began.

Many lumbermen observed the destructive nature of the "cutout and leave" practice and became interested in developing a forestry program. The leader of this effort was Henry Hardtner of the Urania Lumber Company. Some felt that his vision of reforestation was foolish, but he persisted and convinced others that there was a future in second-growth forests.

The George Vanderbilt estate near Asheville, NC, hosted the first forestry program in the United States and still manages forestry holdings. (Photo from Biltmore Estate Web site)

INDIVIDUALS WHO LED RESTORATION OF THE SOUTH'S FORESTS

Early efforts focused on reforestation of the denuded forest lands. But, it was apparent that many other issues needed to be addressed, for example, the role of fire in forest management and the economics of second-growth forestry. So, these early efforts are grouped into the several categories for discussion. Individuals who led restoration efforts will be discussed by category of their contributions.

The individuals selected for focus in this document were not only major contributors to the restoration effort, but they were persons where adequate information could be located for inclusion in this document. Presented will be biographies and accomplishments of about 50 individuals who made significant differences in recovery of the South. Accomplishments for each topic area will be briefly discussed as an overview. Two individuals (H.H. Chapman and P.C. Wakeley) made significant contributions in more than one area and appear twice in descriptions of their accomplishments.

THE COMING OF FORESTRY TO THE SOUTH

As the rapid decimation of forest land occurred, few envisioned that restoration of the forests was feasible. However, Henry Hardtner of the Urania Lumber Company observed that second-growth forests might have potential. He led an effort to convince other mill owners that there was economic potential in young pine stands. Others began to support the ideal of reforestation either by natural regeneration or by tree planting.

Many of the early sawmill enterprises were closed during the late 1920s or 1930s. However, some family owned mills learned from the demonstrations of potential value of their forest land and investing in it. Some of these privately owned family operations continue even today.

A slow influx of trained foresters into the South began with the establishment of the Southern and Appalachian Forest Experiment Stations. These foresters partnered with individuals who developed a practical interest in reforestation. This collaboration of effort started a rapid development of ideas and technology that began the reforestation effort and quickly expanded into other efforts.

One of these early efforts that made a major impact on the development of new forest industry in the South was the initiation of the Southern Forest Survey. This project set the stage for the return of forest industry to the South.

Father of Forestry in the South

HENRY E. HARDTNER

Until the end of the 1800s, pine forests in the West Gulf region remained virtually untouched. But, as the harvest of northern pine forests was exhausted, northern and eastern industrialists moved to the South to invest in the rapidly developing lumber industry. Expansion of railroads made transportation to national markets feasible. The period from 1900 to 1920 was one of big mills. These two decades became a "golden period" for investors, mostly out-of-staters who reaped profits with a cutout and get-out approach. They had little concern for leaving the forests as barren cutover stump wastelands, and they were not concerned about land and resource conservation. Many believed that reestablishment of forests was impossible and that the land would be converted to range or agricultural use.

Henry Hardtner (left), a native of Pineville, LA, founded the Urania timber and sawmill enterprise that lasted 100 years.

7

A few native Louisianans became involved in this lumbering industry. At age 21, Henry Hardtner of Pineville, LA, entered the lumbering scene in 1892 with $1,000 capital. Hardtner quickly parlayed his investment into a small sawmill 30 miles north of Alexandria, LA. In 1896, Hardtner established a mill at a site in Louisiana that he named Urania. To provide access to new tracts of timber, a railroad was built. Although it was only 8 miles long, Hardtner listed the Natchez, Urania and Ruston Railroad on his letterhead. As president, he enjoyed pass privileges on other lines.

Hardtner began to recognize that cutover lands were a serious problem. He enjoyed the woods part of the company's operation and began thoughtful observation of the cutover stands. His growing belief that a second crop of trees could be grown profitably after the virgin timber was cut was ridiculed by others. However, he began a practice of leaving trees smaller than 12 inches and he insisted on leaving four seed trees per acre. Gambling that cutover lands could be brought back into production, he began to buy cutover tracts at $1 per acre. As his belief grew stronger, he initiated a primitive fire protection system and began to fence young longleaf pine stands to protect them from the rooting of open range hogs.

Although Hardtner had no formal forestry training, he read widely about forestry and soon began crusading for the forestry cause. He sought professional forestry advice, one of the first lumbermen to do so. In 1909, the Forest Service sent W.W. Ashe, and later W.R. Mattoon, to assist Hardtner. It is interesting to note that Hardtner's ideas on reforestation were ahead of professional knowledge. However, Ashe and Mattoon gave credibility to Hardtner's actions.

Hardtner's leadership in conservation began to be recognized. In 1910, he led a Commission of Natural Resources that proposed a six-point forestry program. Although it took three decades to implement the recommendations, they became the "cornerstone of forestry in Louisiana."

One of the approved actions was the establishment of State reforestation contracts. These contracts for up to 40 years, allowed assessment of cutover land at a low value for tax purposes, provided that timber was grown and maintained on the lands. Hardtner signed the first reforestation contract in 1913, placing 25,719 acres of Urania Lumber Company's land under a 40-year contract. This forest reserve became an experimental site where forestry reforestation practices where developed.

Elected to the Louisiana Legislature as both Representative and Senator, Hardtner had great influence on the reforestation of cutover lands within the State and on the development of forest practices across the South.

Hardtner's father was a shoemaker in Alexandria, LA. Henry was quoted as saying, "I was born in the forests and have had close association with them since childhood. What I know about them cannot be learned in schools or colleges. To me they are as humans and I know trees as I try to know men." This desire to know more about reforestation potential of cutover lands led him to invite, in 1917, the Yale University Forestry School to conduct its spring field course for students in Urania, LA. This association went on for decades and resulted in many of America's leading foresters receiving training there.

Philip Wakeley spoke of Hardtner as a shrewd businessman who had a grasp of the future. By 1924, Hardtner's Urania mill was sawing second-growth fixed-assessment timber. Wakeley is quoted as saying, "He had an old rattle trap mill and Urania, the town, was nothing to look at... Around Urania was the center of the Yale camp for years, and having started this program he utilized the full advice of Chapman and other members of the Yale faculty. So, there was a nucleus, a focus of happy affection, so to speak, at Urania, dating back roughly to 1912."

Hardtner's enthusiasm and persistence in the field of advanced forest management caused many people to take a second look at their timber stands and the reclamation of their cutover lands. Urania became the location for persons interested in forestry and conservation lumbering to learn of forest management. The impact of the demonstrations and visits is impossible to measure, but they contributed to the recognition of Hardtner as the "father of southern forestry."

References

Burns, A.C. 1978. Henry E. Hardtner, Louisiana's first conservationist. Journal of Forest History. 22: 79-85.

Burns, A.C. 1978. Henry Ernest Hardtner—A lumberman's vision of reforestation. Forests & People. 28(4): 17-20, 39-41.

Clark, T.D. 1984. The greening of the South: The recovery of land and forest. Lexington, KY: The University Press of Kentucky. 168 p.

Demmon, E.L. 1943. The South's forest frontier and the war. Social Forces. 21(4): 397-405.

Demmon, E.L. 1935. Henry E. Hardtner. Journal of Forestry. 33: 885-886.

Kerr, E.F. 1953. Louisiana's State story, Part 1. American Forests. 59(2): 24-26, 55.

Mattoon, W.R. 1939. Dedication address to Henry E. Hardtner. Journal of Forestry. 37: 761-762.

Early "Transient" Foresters in the South

As late as the mid-1920s, there were fewer than 20 professionally trained foresters in the entire South. With exception of these who had attended the Biltmore Forestry School in North Carolina, most of these were recent graduates of forestry schools established in the North. However, before these graduates were in the field there were a few early transient foresters that did invaluable work in the South although they were located in Washington, DC. Three of these traveled the South over a period of years in the early 1900s as employees of the Forest Service. The need for forestry expertise was beginning to be recognized and these individuals greatly influenced the development of forestry practices in the South as well as in other regions. These individuals were recruited because of their unique capabilities.

WILLIAM W. ASHE

Ashe was a native of North Carolina (born in 1872) and was trained as a pioneer naturalist, not a trained forester. He attended the University of North Carolina and Cornell University from 1891 to 1892. Ashe participated with Gifford Pinchot and Carl Schenck at the Biltmore Estate in the first experiments conducted in silviculture and forest management. He wrote the first comprehensive treatise on loblolly pine in 1915, worked for the North Carolina Geological Survey as a forester from 1891 to 1909 and greatly influenced the establishment of forestry within the State.

As a forestry practitioner, he encouraged Charles H. Herty, then a chemist at the University of North Carolina, to conduct an analysis of North Carolina's turpentine and resin extracting procedures. Ashe suggested that a better method of gathering gum should be sought, a suggestion that led to the invention and perfection of the Herty cup for resin collection.

He was a forest specialist hired in 1909 by the Forest Service, and it was largely through his efforts and his knowledge and experience of forest conditions that the national forests in the South were established. Ashe also was one of the few individuals having any professional forestry knowledge when Chief Forester Pinchot sent him in 1910 to provide guidance to Henry Hardtner of the Urania Lumber Company.

Ashe was an outstanding botanical authority on forest trees and vegetation and was an advocate of forest cover on water quality. He was the man who determined tentative boundaries for national forest purchase units on land that in those days nobody really wanted. That was usually tax delinquent, cutover land.

For example, he was the Forest Service representative interacting with Caroline Dormon who was leading the effort to establish a national forest in Louisiana. He was a very quiet individual and did not have much to say, but he was an excellent observer.

Ashe's illness and death in 1932 significantly slowed the effort to establish national forests in Louisiana and a number of other Southern States. His botanical work in the South was authoritative. He made significant contributions to botany, dendrology, and early ecological work in the Eastern United States. One of the most enduring personal contributions was his dogged campaign to help secure the famous Weeks Law in 1911 that provided for purchase of land to establish national forests.

Ashe was highly respected and after his death the Forest Service tree nursery at Brooklyn, MS, was named in his honor. His extensive plant collection, which contained over 20,000 dried specimens, was acquired after his death by the Coker Herbarium at the University of North Carolina.

W.W. Ashe was a noted botanist.

Wilbur R. (Matty) Mattoon

Wilbur R. (Matty) Mattoon was the pioneer extension forester working out of the Forest Service's Washington, DC, office who was in charge of Federal forestry education in the South. Although most of his work was with State extension foresters in the Southern States, he made real contributions to southern forestry because of his publications and speeches. Mattoon was widely known and devoted most of his attention to small landowners.

Matty Mattoon provided forestry information to extension specialists across the South.

Mattoon was one of the best writers in the Forest Service on forestry matters. He wrote bulletins on the southern pines and cypress that were easy for people to understand. In 1922, he published the first comprehensive bulletin on longleaf pine. Through his writings, many folks learned more about forestry than they would have otherwise. The information contained in the publications was used by extension foresters as a guide to improve forestry practices throughout the region.

In all of Mattoon's writings and speeches, he was optimistic about the possibilities of timber growing in the South. He was a friendly, pleasant, and courteous individual always making a favorable impression during meetings. He was a good example of a man in the Forest Service working in the public interest—not primarily for pay, but to make a difference.

Mattoon could take findings from a research organization and put them into simple language that a farmer could understand. His responsibility covered a lot of territory, and he had a lot of influence in getting forestry started where there had been no previous forestry program. In some States, there was a State extension forester before a State forestry organization was established. As an example, Arkansas had an extension forester for several years before it had a State forestry department.

Austin Cary

Austin Cary was a nationally known forestry pioneer who worked for the Forest Service, State forestry organizations, forestry schools, and private companies. Born in Maine in 1865, Cary entered Bowdoin University at 18 and obtained two degrees by 1890. He was awarded an honorary doctorate by Bowdoin in 1922. Cary had early training in the Maine woods where lumbering was the primary activity of his New England family.

Cary worked for a number of early forestry related businesses, traveled to Europe to learn of their forestry practices, and published numerous publications related to thinning, naval stores, and fire issues. Always, he approached these issues with a businessman's view. He became a pioneer on the practical side of forestry. In 1910, he was appointed as logging engineer for the Forest Service in Washington, DC.

In 1917, Cary first visited the South in his new capacity. He came to realize the South's potential as a major timber-growing region in the United States. At a time when most lumbermen saw no future in owning cutover forest land, Cary began a campaign to convince them of the potential of forestry. Cary would not spend time with underlings, but

Austin Cary promoted the practice of forestry to influential lumbermen.

would charge into the office of the general manager or company president. Always carrying an axe, he would take the men into the woods. He would not hesitate to cut down a tree or two just to illustrate its growth rate by counting annual rings. Observations such as these made a deep impression on many of the lumbermen and they had great respect for Cary.

Cary, a shaggy, red-bearded New England Yankee, would come back repeatedly selling them on forestry. They liked and enjoyed him and over time he convinced them to begin forestry programs. Cary spent his winters in the South, working out of Florida and returning north during the summer. Although Cary was a member of the Forest Service, he was so independent that they had little control over him. The Washington Office of the Forest Service rarely kept track of where he was or what he was doing. They understood, however, the value of his forest extension work and talent in interesting lumbermen in forestry.

He was a rugged individualist and a nonconformist in social customs as in forestry. William Greeley, who was an early Chief Forester of the Forest Service, remembers inviting Cary as a dinner guest soon after he married. When completing the dinner, Cary returned to the living room, shed his coat, unbuttoned his vest, and stretched out on Greeley's sofa. Soon he kicked off his shoes and began a running fire of comment on current publications and doings in forestry. Greeley's bride looked at Cary with astonishment. Little did she know that this was the custom of Cary after dinner, regardless of location.

Cary was a remarkable teacher. He endeared himself to students by his pithy, homely ways of putting things and by his practical, down to earth Yankee mind. He was one of the great early leaders in American forestry, not in official organizations or programs, but as an individualist in the woods. As a roving missionary in the South, he laid much of the groundwork for the piney woods forestry of today.

He foresaw the great promise in the pine lands of the South. Judged solely as a forester, Cary deserves the highest rank, but his role as a champion of the South demands even greater recognition. The progress of southern forestry and forest industries unmistakably bear the imprint of his work. Heyward (1955) states "Forest history will record the South's fond remembrance of, and respectful gratitude to, the 'Yankee peddler of forestry,' Austin Cary."

References

Ashe, W.W. 1915. Loblolly or North Carolina pine. Bulletin 24. Raleigh, NC: North Carolina Geological and Economic Survey. 176 p.

Clark, T.D. 1984. The greening of the South: The recovery of land and forest. Lexington, KY: The University of Kentucky Press. 168 p.

Greeley, W.B. 1955. Austin Cary as I knew him. American Forestry. 61(5): 30.

Heyward, F. 1955. Austin Cary: Yankee peddler in forestry. American Forests. 61(5): 29-30, 43-44; 61(6): 28-29, 52-53.

Heyward, F. 1958. History of industrial forestry in the South. The Colonel William B. Greeley lectures in industrial forestry. Seattle, WA: University of Washington, College of Forestry. 50 p.

Mattoon, W.R. 1922. Longleaf pine. Bulletin 1061. Washington, DC: U.S. Department of Agriculture. 50 p.

Maunder, E.R. 1977. Voices from the past: Reflections of four foresters; Inman F. Eldredge, Elwood L. Demmon, Walter J. Damtoft, Clinton H. Coulter. Santa Cruz, CA: Forest History Society, Inc. 252 p.

White, R.R. 1961. Austin Cary, the father of southern forestry. Forest History. 5(1): 3-4.

Reforestation Pioneer
Philip C. (Phil) Wakeley

The period from 1900 to 1920 marked the "golden" era of lumbering in Louisiana; an era when native forests were harvested with a "cut-out and get-out" attitude. Large and small sawmills harvested these forests with no thought of reforestation. Many of these companies abandoned their cutover lands, and ownership of them reverted to the State when taxes were not paid. However, a few individuals began to see the economic potential of reforesting the cutover land, and Henry Hardtner of the Urania Lumber Company led this effort.

Hardtner's efforts at Urania focused on leaving a few trees per acre for natural regeneration. His efforts caught the attention of Great Southern at Bogalusa, LA. Great Southern was one of the largest mills in the South,

Phil Wakeley photographed in 1962 late in his career. By this time, he had garnered regional, national, and international recognition for his contributions to southern forestry.

running four 8-foot band saws that could produce one million board feet of lumber every 24 hours and did so for more than two decades. Great Southern hired J.K. Johnson, one of the first industrial foresters, to begin efforts to reforest some of their cutover land by seeding and planting techniques.

The Forest Service established the Southern Forest Experiment Station (Southern Station) in 1921 with its headquarters in New Orleans, LA. Reforestation was recognized as one of the greatest needs in the South. Three years later, the Southern Station recruited Philip C. Wakeley. Wakeley received a forestry degree in 1923 from Cornell University—the first 4-year school of forestry in the United States. Upon arriving in New Orleans, LA, the New York native was assigned to Bogalusa, LA to establish a cooperative reforestation program with Great Southern.

The cooperative effort between Phil Wakeley and Great Southern was very productive. Great Southern developed an operational nursery that also served as a research facility. Not only did J.K. Johnson and his ranger, "Red" Bateman, provide local technical support, but they helped acclimate Wakeley to the South. In order to give Wakeley an experience with chiggers, Bateman led Wakeley to sit on the ground to eat his lunch. So, on his first day in the field, Wakeley was able to get acquainted with redbug bites.

The Great Southern staff and Wakeley worked together for about 10 years. During this time, Wakeley was able to develop and compile rudimentary guidelines for producing and planting pine seedlings. With the onset of the Great Depression in the early 1930s, Great Southern went into receivership. About the same time, the Kisatchie National Forest and the Civilian Conservation Corps (CCC) established the Stuart Nursery north of Alexandria, LA, near Pollock. The reforestation emphasis shifted from Great Southern to the Stuart Nursery.

Wakeley documented his preliminary research in a U.S. Department of Agriculture Technical Bulletin that was used extensively across the South in the reforestation programs carried out by the CCC during the 1930s. Moreover, the availability of labor from the CCC program at the Stuart Nursery allowed Wakeley and his colleagues to conduct additional large scale research outplantings. Nearly 700,000 seedlings were planted in research studies on the Palustris Experimental Forest that was established by Wakeley for this purpose.

In 1954, Wakeley published the results of his reforestation work into the book "Planting the Southern Pines." This publication provided the information necessary to establish successful reforestation programs. It is probably the most cited forestry publication in the South, and is still frequently cited today though having been out of print for decades.

Phil Wakeley was a keen observer and keeper of meticulous records. Even after retirement, he could be called upon to provide specific locations for individual studies or trees from genetics outplantings made decades earlier. His career covered 40 years, all with the Southern Station in New Orleans, LA. He was recognized by a number of awards: U.S. Department of Agriculture Superior Service Award, elected by Society of American Foresters as Fellow and for the Barrington Moore Award for Biological Research. Phil is recognized across the South, as well as nationally and internationally, for his contributions to restoration of southern forest ecosystems. He probably contributed more to the reforestation of the South than any other individual. His work facilitated the change of face of the South from cutover desolation to productive pine forests.

References

Wakeley, P.C. 1964. A biased history of the Southern Forest Experiment Station through fiscal year 1933. Unpublished document. New Orleans, LA: On file with: USDA Forest Service, Southern Research Station, Forest Management Research, Pineville, LA 71360.

Wakeley, P.C. 1978. The adolescence of forestry research in the South. Journal of Forest History. 22(7): 136-145.

Pioneer Nursery Specialist and Silviculturist Extraordinary

F.O. (RED) BATEMAN

Soon after Henry Hardtner, president of the Urania Lumber Company, began efforts to reforest his company's lands, Great Southern, headquartered in Bogalusa, LA, became interested in reforestation. Great Southern was one of the larger mills in the South, and had the financial backing of the Goodyear family of Pennsylvania.

The Great Southern company began an aggressive forestry program in 1919-20. Col. William H. Sullivan, general manager, named F.O. Bateman as head ranger. Bateman was known as "Red" for his florid complexion. Unlike his younger brother, Bryant Bateman, long of the faculty of the School of Forestry at Louisiana State University, Bateman's formal education extended only to the ninth grade. However, he had a remarkable talent for extracting both factual information and constructive ideas from the many professional foresters with whom his work brought him in contact.

From the start of Great Southern's artificial reforestation at Bogalusa, LA Bateman was the prime mover in developing planting principles and techniques. By 1922-23, two growing seasons before Philip Wakeley arrived at the Forest Service, Southern Forest Research Station to conduct reforestation research, Red had worked out the essentials of the general practice still employed today—slit planting of bare-rooted seedlings grown at moderate seedbed

F.O. "Red" Bateman standing by a Tung-oil tree. (Photo from C.W. Goodyear collection)

densities in the nursery without shade. He developed a planting tool (or "dibble") that is still used to plant pine seedlings. The 6- by 8-foot spacing he chose as most suitable and economical for southern pines was the almost universal standard throughout the South for decades. Before the Great Depression halted his company's planting operations, Bateman had planted 12,700 acres. With only one exception (the Biltmore estate in North Carolina), there was no other successful southern pine plantation of more than 100 acres.

Bateman's ingenuity was described by Wakeley when he remarked to Bateman that it was a pity that the persistent wings of longleaf pine seeds prevented drill-sowing that species on nursery beds. By noon, Bateman asked Wakeley to stop by the nursery. During the morning Bateman had designed a drill seeder that worked with longleaf pine. It was a wooden trough 5 feet long to fit across nursery beds. It was hinged to open at the bottom and drop seeds on the bed. A pair of tall, curved handles at each end permitted opening it without stooping or kneeling, which made the device easy to use. This seeder designed in a morning resulted in marked improvement in the uniformity and quality of longleaf pine nursery stock.

Not only did Bateman determine how to plant southern pines effectively, in anticipation of a bumper fall crop of longleaf pine, he persuaded Col. W.H. Sullivan to let him fence 15,000 acres of burned forest land to protect the area from hogs. The 1920 crop exceeded all

expectations, and Bateman's activity resulted in establishing longleaf seedlings on 10,000 acres, all from a single seed crop—a notable achievement.

Another aspect of Bateman's early work was the prevention and suppression of fire on company lands. Bateman observed the fire was needed to prepare areas for seed fall or planting, but that seedlings were killed by fire while in the cotyledon stage. As they developed they became tolerant to fire.

As an example of Bateman's practical approach, he described to a couple of young researchers why direct seeding would not work. This was decades before repellents were found to protect seeds from bird and rodent depredation. Wakeley (1976) quotes Bateman's comments on his final vain attempts to direct seed in plowed furrows:

> *When we went out to start seeding, there was a pheellock [field lark or meadowlark] sittin' on a fence, he whistled, and up come fifty more pheellocks. We went down the furrows, dropping five longleaf seeds every six feet. The pheellocks follered us down the furrows and, gentlemen, when we got to the end of the furrows, there wasn't a damn thing left in the furrows but bird-s—t!*

Bateman was an untiring and marvelously keen observer with far above-average ability to reason about what he saw. These personal traits and his accomplishments make him, as Wakeley described, "one of the greatest silviculturists the South has known." Not only was Red Bateman a great silviculturist, he was remembered by Charles Goodyear as a tung-orchardist and a trainer of pointers to hunt quail. Red died at age 46 from a heart attack.

References

Wakeley, Philip C. 1976. F.O. (Red) Bateman, pioneer silviculturist. Journal of Forest History. 20(2): 91-99.

F.O. Bateman's seeder for sowing longleaf pine seeds in the nursery in operation. This simple tool significantly improved the quality of nursery longleaf pine seedlings.

The Nation's First Industrial Forester?

J.T. (Jake) Johnson

J.T (Jake) Johnson, called by many as the "granddaddy of Louisiana's foresters," contributed an immeasurable quality of skill, labor, and ingenuity to the rebuilding of the South's great pine forests. Johnson was born in Washington Parish, LA. Although he had no formal forestry training, Johnson had obtained a teaching certificate after taking a public examination in 1896.

Johnson joined the old Great Southern company of Bogalusa, LA in 1912. The Great Southern in its heyday was capable of devouring a million board feet of timber through its four band saws every 24 hours. The old growth timber in Louisiana and Mississippi was rapidly being depleted. Col. A.C. Goodyear, one of the founders of Great Southern, proposed a reforestation plan in about 1918 or 1919. Since it was recommended that a local person be chosen for the task, W.H. Sullivan, vice-president and general manager, asked Johnson, "How'd you like to be our new forester, Jake?" This greatly pleased Johnson who lived and practiced conservation. Johnson was told to "proceed without delay."

But, there were no seedlings to plant. There was not even a tree nursery (that came 2 years later). An 800-acre area had been clearcut several years earlier. Without seed trees to restock the site, it was treeless and covered with a heavy stand of native grasses. Jake thought that if the area was burned to reduce the grasses and fenced to exclude grazing the area might be ideal for direct seeding. Loblolly pine cones were collected and seed extracted and dried. Johnson believed scarification of the site would enhance germination and survival. So, a crew of employees with mules and farm plows turned shallow furrows about 8 feet apart. After harrowing the furrow berms to reduce soil clods, 10 loblolly pine seeds were sown every 6 feet within the furrow. The seeding was a success: at age 1, the stand averaged about 3,000 trees per acre. This stand became the Nation's earliest industrial direct seeding.

Johnson established a one-half-acre pine nursery in 1921-22 across from the city hall in Bogalusa, LA—believed to be the first pine nursery in the South. Other nurseries followed, and under the leadership of Johnson, about 30,000 acres were fenced and reforested. For planting, Jake initially used a Model T Ford axle shaft. Although he had

Jake Johnson was considered to be the first industrial forester in the South, if not the Nation.

success, others thought a better tool should be developed. So, Jake and his staff designed the present day "dibble" for planting of nursery seedlings.

One of Johnson's major roles was to "sell" reforestation to the local community. Protecting the seedlings from fire was a greater challenge than growing the planting stock. Open land was typically burned every year to improve open grazing, reduce insect problems, facilitate collection of "lighter" pine knots, and so forth. He believed that the company had to "change people's minds about setting fire

Great Southern Lumber Company's forest tree nursery established in 1921-22 across from the city hall in Bogalusa, LA. This probably was the earliest tree nursery established in the South.

to the woodlands." He pointed out that "we'd never have trees again after the big mill cuts 'em unless we stopped the fires." Jake spent time in the schools (he was a school board member) to discuss the issues, and he felt that the idea of reforestation would "take root in the rising generation—and it has, too."

In the mid-1950s, Gaylord Container Corporation, the successor to Great Southern, had about 100,000 acres of pine plantations. This reforestation success is attributed to Johnson and his farsighted policy of pine plantations that was developed in the early 1920s. In his advanced years, Johnson said, "I consider my greatest accomplishment of my forestry career in the country was that of helping create a condition favorable to the growing of trees. The big thing is to protect them into maturity. This, in the old days, was the biggest job."

In appreciation of Johnson's contributions to the early development of reforestation practices, Philip Wakeley of the Southern Station led an effort to name a tract of the Palustris Experiment Forest, a part of the Kisatchie National Forest near Alexandria, LA, in honor of Johnson. This designation was done to recognize the contributions of this pioneer forestry practitioner to the reforestation of the South's forest lands.

References

Campbell, T.E. 1976. The Nation's oldest industrial direct seeding. Forests & People. 26(3): 22-24.

Garrison, P.M. 1952. Building an industry on cutover land. Journal of Forestry. 50(3): 185-187.

Landry, B. 1953. Jake Johnson. Forests & People. 3(3): 28-31, 45.

The First Forest Survey of the South

The establishment of the Forest Survey in the South was a major accomplishment, a catalyst for developing forest industry throughout the entire area. Second-growth forests were the pride of early foresters, but their nature, usefulness and location were in question. The Forest Survey was undertaken to answer the questions of those interested in investing in forestry.

The Forest Survey was remarkable in many aspects. The plan was well thought out, and the first survey of the entire South was finished in 4 years.

The structure of the survey developed in the early 1930s is still used today. The Forest Survey remains one of the important functions of the Forest Service.

INMAN F. (CAP) ELDREDGE

In the late 1920s, some timberland owners and managers began to understand that second-growth pine forests beginning to develop across the South could be profitable. A number of pioneers began to promote reforestation of cutover forests. Much of the initial effort was due to individuals like Henry Hardtner at Urania Lumber Company, Col. W.H. Sullivan at Great Southern Lumber Company, and Austin Cary of the Forest Service. However, products that could be profitably made from young pine trees were needed. Charles H. Herty, a noted chemist in Georgia, demonstrated that newsprint could be made from young southern pines and began a promotional effort to convince southern landowners that there was value in these young stands. The next step was to determine if there was sufficient raw material to support constructing paper mills.

The Forest Service, Southern Station assigned I.F. (Cap) Eldredge the task of surveying the South to determine the extent of pine forests suitable for forest industry. Eldredge was fully capable of leading this monumental effort. He attended Clemson University for a while, studying engineering, but in 1903 he entered the forestry program at Biltmore Forest School. Eldredge was hired by the Forest Service in 1906 and worked in the West for a few years. In 1909, he was temporarily assigned to the newly created national forests in Florida. In the absence of the named supervisor, Eldredge served in that capacity for 8 years administering about a half million acres of timberland.

I.F. "Cap" Eldredge was very effective in advocating the value of the forest survey.

15

In 1917, at the outbreak of World War I, Eldredge was commissioned and served in the Army as captain in the 10th Engineers (Forestry), a pioneer forestry unit, in southern France. Here he got his nickname "Cap" that was used the rest of his life.

For a period beginning in 1926, Eldredge was employed to purchase and manage the Suwannee Forest in the longleaf pine region of southeast Georgia. This 208,000-acre tract was owned by the Superior Pine Products Company of Fargo, GA. The town of Fargo was abandoned by the previous owner and was purchased by Eldredge's company. It had become a sump into which all the hard characters of Florida and Georgia ended up when pursued by the law. Fargo had no law enforcement and was known as "Bad Man's Fargo." Most of the employees worked in naval stores or turpentine chipping camps and were a tough lot.

However, under Eldredge's guidance, Fargo was tamed and the Suwannee Forest became a proving ground for many forest practices including planting, thinning, and prescribed burning. Eldredge was quoted as saying, "Turpentine operators were the greatest, ablest, and most energetic set of wood-burners that the Lord has ever smiled upon."

After several years, Eldredge returned to the Forest Service, and in 1932 he was selected to head the Southern Forest Survey. The survey was more than a gigantic timber cruise. As important as data on total wood volume by individual species, was information on industrial use, mortality, and net growth. For the first time, there was information for each State on the ratio of growth to drain. Industry for the first time had factual data pertaining to the timber resource.

Conducting the survey was a massive undertaking. A system of compass lines ran 10 miles apart across each State from Tennessee southward to the tip of Florida. At every 660 feet on these lines, plots were established and a great deal of information was taken. Fortunately for the Research Station, many of the best timber men in the South were available to work on the survey because of the Great Depression. The survey started at the Atlantic coast and ended in the prairies of Texas. The field effort was completed in 4 years, although analysis and publication of the data took longer.

The survey was carried out ably and vigorously under difficult conditions. For example, it was reported that swamps near Grand Lake and Morgan City, LA, were traversed generally on hands and knees. Releases on results were eagerly sought and survey's reputation was made and that of the Southern Station greatly enhanced.

The Forest Survey began just as interest in forestry was developing and forest industries became the survey's best supporters. The Forest Survey probably had more to do with the rapid expansion of southern forestry in the 1930s than any other project.

Eldredge had a remarkable ability for understanding and knowing how to work with people on all levels. A native of South Carolina he spoke the language of southerners, Eldredge was one of few southerners who at the time had gone into forestry. Most foresters in the South at the time were from the North. Eldredge knew Southern customs and way of life, and he was a technical forester with a national reputation. However, Wakeley noted that Eldredge had a devilish sense of humor. As acting station director, Eldredge sent Wakeley to Washington, DC, on a $3 per diem (the cheapest hotel room was $3.50), while Eldredge toured small towns in the South on a $5 per diem in connection with the Forest Survey.

PHILIP R. (PHIL) WHEELER

While Eldredge oversaw the first Forest Survey, he did not have the training or expertise to develop plans for the survey nor for analysis of the data collected. It was Philip R. Wheeler who led aspects of this important undertaking.

Wheeler, a native of Grand Rapids, MI, and 1930 graduate of the University of Michigan, provided the Southern Station with the capability to produce products that forestry investors needed to make decisions. When Wheeler arrived at the Station in 1931, he joined the group planning the survey. Another in the planning group was Roy Chapman, who provided guidance on sampling techniques and analytic procedures. However, it was Wheeler who developed the practical field techniques and effective analysis and dissemination of results.

Phil Wheeler (right) with Dr. R.S. Campbell, range scientist.

Wheeler pioneered the use of computers in analysis of the data from the survey and led development of the forest survey technology following World War II. During the war, he served in important Coast Guard commands such as Captain of the Port of New Orleans and overseas duty in the Pacific. In 1947, he was appointed Chief, Division of Forest Management Research, and in 1952 was promoted to Chief of the Division of Forest Economics for the Southern Station.

Wheeler was energetic, tenacious, and thorough in the projects that came his way. Tall, thin, and brisk of speech, he gained wide respect for his leadership. He received the Department of Agriculture Superior Service Award, the Schlich Medal, and Fellow status by the Society of American Foresters.

After retirement from the Forest Service in 1962, Wheeler worked for the Southern Pine Association as analyst for the Southern Forest Resource Committee. In this role, he led development of the famous document entitled, "The South's Third Forest." This report laid out what has been described as the most ambitious program for timber resource development in history.

The Third Forest report called for doubling timber growth in the South prior to the year 2000 to meet anticipated needs for forest products, recreation, and other essentials. The report resulted in incentives and assistance for small landowners, who hold 70 percent of the region's forest land.

Wheeler played an important role in providing data through effective analysis and dissemination which fostered the development of forest industry in the South.

References

Anon. 1963. Inman F. Eldredge (1883-1963). Journal of Forestry. 61(6): 470.

Anon. 1970. Faces of Forestry—Philip R. Wheeler. Forests & People. 20(1): 33-34.

Maunder, E.R. 1977. Voices from the South: recollections of four foresters; Inman F. Eldredge, Elwood L. Demmon, Walter H. Damtoft, Clinton H. Coulter. Santa Cruz, CA: Forest History Society, Inc. 252 p.

Wakeley, P.C. 1964. A biased history of the Southern Forest Experiment Station through fiscal year 1933. Unpublished document. New Orleans, LA: On file with: USDA Forest Service, Southern Research Station, Forest Management Research, Pineville, LA 73160.

ADMINISTRATION

Administrators of early forestry organizations were notable by their strong will and personality. Most had advantage of some level of formal education. This probably gave them the incentive to take on major responsibilities.

Some of these administrators were determined to maximize profits and move on to other challenges. Others had the same drive to accomplish success, but understood that they should be compassionate to their employees and built meaningful collaborative efforts.

Great Southern Lumber Company
William H. (Col. Bill) Sullivan

William H. (Col. Bill) Sullivan, the vice-president and general manager of Great Southern, was born in St. Catherine, Ontario, in 1864. Soon after graduating in 1884 from the Bryant and Stratton Business School, Sullivan met Frank and Charles Goodyear of Buffalo, NY. The Goodyear brothers were so impressed with Sullivan they hired him on the spot and gave him the responsibility of perfecting plans for and constructing a huge sawmill complex in Louisiana. Meanwhile, the Goodyears turned their attention to finances and to plans for the city of Bogalusa, LA that was to eventually house 15,000 people.

Credit for conceiving the plan of converting a lumber camp into a self-governing city is due to Sullivan, its designer and builder, and to the liberal-mindedness of Frank and Charles Goodyear. Aided with wise counsel and generosity, they approved the initial expenditures by the company to make the idea effective.

Sullivan moved to Bogalusa, LA in 1907 with his wife, Elizabeth Calkins, of Buffalo, NY. Under his supervision, the Great Southern erected the first mill in the World constructed of steel. It was also the world's largest with a 24-hour capacity of 1 million board feet of lumber. The mill began operation in 1908.

Col. W.H. Sullivan was a remarkable leader and visionary. He led the development of one of the largest sawmills in the South.

In 1920, Great Southern Lumber Company reforestation efforts began with this direct seeding of loblolly pine on seed beds created by plowing berms with mules. This was the first successful large-scale effort.

This mammoth plant was the basis for building the attractive city of Bogalusa, LA. Sullivan extended the business to paper making which assured continued growth through diversified manufacturing. Sullivan was the first and long-term mayor of the city, and he worked aggressively to develop economic possibilities for the region. Proposed and developed were a canning factory, culture of Satsuma oranges, planting of Tung tree orchards for the production of Tung oil, and numerous other programs that provided economic stability. However, development of the Great Southern's massive reforestation effort was the program that brought national and international recognition.

It is not clear whether Sullivan conceived or merely executed the early forestry activities of the company. At any rate, he was in charge of those historic accomplishments. In 1920, the historic reforestation program was initiated. Inspired by Henry Hardtner's pioneering work at Urania, the company decided to plant 800 acres of cutover land immediately adjacent to Bogalusa, LA. Unable to obtain seedlings, the company decided to direct seed the area with loblolly pine. Seeds were sown on ridges made with mule teams and plows. The effort was successful and is believed to be the first large scale commercial establishment of forest species in the United States.

This success led the company to begin an aggressive reforestation program. Key to its success was development of nursery and planting technology. Sullivan hired a forester (J.K. (Jake) Johnson) and ranger (F.O. (Red) Bateman) to oversee this effort. He provided the resources to make the program successful.

In 1924, a collaborative effort was established with the Forest Service, Southern Station to develop reforestation technology. At Sullivan's direction, Great Southern planted thousands of acres of pine seedlings. As a result of experimentation and observation made during the progress of this vast project, much general knowledge on artificial reforestation was accumulated. Much of the information published in Philip Wakeley's 1954 classic "Planting the Southern Pines" was developed as a result of this joint operational research effort.

Sullivan died in 1929. The Great Southern sawmill closed in 1938 as a result of the economic problems resulting from the Great Depression and insufficient old-growth forests remaining to maintain its operation. However, Sullivan's vision in diversifying the company resulted in the 1937 merger into the Gaylord Container Corporation paper mill and its continued operation as a forestry enterprise.

In 1954, the Gaylord Container Corporation, successor to Great Southern, planted its 100 millionth pine seedling in its 110,500-acre forest. This became the largest privately owned man-made forest in North America, and the first planted forest in the country of sufficient size to reach merchantable age. This forest is a lasting testimony to Sullivan's vision and the energy and dedication to carry out his vision in a practical way.

References

Anon. 1954. Out of the pages of history steps a new man-made forest. Forests & People. 4(2): 32-34, 38.

Garrison, P.M. 1952. Building an industry on cutover land. Journal of Forestry. 50(3): 185-187.

Heyward, F. 1963. Col. W.H. Sullivan—Paul Bunyan of Louisiana forestry. Forests & People. 13(1): 20.

Goodyear, C.W. 1950. Bogalusa Story. Buffalo, NY. Privately printed. {http://freepages.genealogy.rootsweb.com/~mcclendon/Bogalusa/Bogalusa Story/index.html}.

Southern Forest Experiment Station

When the Forest Service established the Southern Station in New Orleans in 1921, there were only a few professionally trained foresters in the South. With the exception of the Biltmore Forest School in North Carolina, which consisted of 1 year of practical training, there was only one forestry school in the South, established in 1906 at the University of Georgia. Also, by then the Biltmore Forest School had been closed for 8 years. So, staffing of the Southern Station, and the Appalachian Forest Experiment Station that was established at the same time in Asheville, NC, was a challenge. Fortunately, several universities in the North had established forestry programs, for example, Cornell, Yale, Minnesota, and Michigan.

The Southern Station originally was responsible for research in the southern pine types. This included all Coastal Plain areas in Georgia and South Carolina; all of Florida, Alabama, Mississippi, and Louisiana; Texas and Oklahoma as far west as the pine types went; and Arkansas south of the Arkansas River. So, the early employees had a huge area of responsibility. It was not until 1946 that the boundaries of the Experiment Stations were realigned and the Southeastern Forest Experiment Station created to replace the Appalachian Station with its emphasis on mountainous hardwood species.

REGINALD D. (REGGIE) FORBES

Soon after Reginald D. (Reggie) Forbes graduated from the Yale University School of Forestry in 1913, he was hired as Louisiana's first State forester. The Department of Conservation established a forestry division and named Forbes as State forester in October, 1917. Forbes charted his program needs into three categories: (1) fire patrol, (2) railroad fire prevention, and (3) publicity and education.

As forestry efforts expanded, Forbes found need for an assistant and the Department of Conservation approved hiring V.H. Sonderegger as the first assistant State forester. Sonderegger was a graduate of the Biltmore Forest School and was hired in November 1920. In the following year, nine of the proposed ranger positions were filled. During the period of Forbes' tenure, great strides were made in establishing a sound and sensible program in forestry.

In July 1921, Forbes resigned as State forester and became the first director of the Southern Station. Others who were named to the technical staff of the Experiment Station were Lenthal Wyman and W.R. (Billy) Hine. Hine had graduated from Cornell University. He left the station in 1925 to become Louisiana's State forester.

R.D. Forbes had the distinction of being the first State forester of Louisiana and Station Director of the Southern Forest Experiment Station.

By 1924, several additional foresters were added to the staff, and the Station had established five major areas of research. These were (1) growth and yield tables for second-growth stands, (2) influence of fire, (3) naval stores, (4) reproduction cuttings, and (5) reforestation.

At Forbes' own request, he was transferred to Pennsylvania in 1927 to become the director of the newly established Allegheny Forest Experiment Station. He was replaced as director of the Southern Station by E.L. Demmon, who had been assigned to the station 2 years earlier.

Forbes left the Southern Station as it was beginning to gain respect for its contributions to the early development of forestry practices in the South. He played a major role in establishing effective forestry programs at both the State and Federal level. Late in his career he wrote the "Forestry Handbook" that was developed by the Society of American Foresters. The 1955 publication was a major reference book designed for the use of all who had a professional or commercial interest in the forest lands and crops of North America. It was a fitting compilation of his contributions to forestry.

After Forbes retired from the Forest Service, he taught English. He was noted for dressing well and being straitlaced and honest.

ELWOOD L. (DEMMIE) DEMMON

Elwood (Demmie) Demmon was born in 1892. He was assigned to the Southern Station in 1925. A graduate with an AB degree in 1914 and an MSF degree in 1916 from Michigan University's School of Forestry, he had worked for more than 6 years in Sumatra, Dutch East Indies, in tropical forestry—primarily related to management of rubber plantations. Tired of this work, Demmon returned to the United States in 1923 and obtained a temporary job with the Lake States Forest Experiment Station in St. Paul, MN.

When he obtained a permanent position, Elwood was offered a job with the Southern Station in New Orleans, LA. His initial assignment was related to conducting what were called "extensive surveys." This effort was to obtain general information on the growth of timber, effect of fire, and other problems dealing with southern forestry. With the

E.L. Demmon was a noted economist and administrator for the Forest Service.

departure of R.D. Forbes in 1927, Demmon was made director of the Southern Station. He served in this capacity until the summer of 1944.

During Demmon's period of leadership at the Southern Station, remarkable progress was made in a number of areas. One of the first was the publication in 1929 of the "Volume, Yield, and Stand Tables for Second-Growth Southern Pines," which became known to field foresters as Misc. Pub. 50. This document did much to demonstrate the productivity of second-growth forests.

Another significant accomplishment was the improvement in resin yields through naval stores research at Starke, FL. Lenthall Wyman, working on the problem, did a thoroughly sound and practical job by reducing the streak size from 1 inch high and deep to half of an inch. This and other techniques improved resin yields and increased profits.

Ralph M. Lindgren's work on blue stain of lumber gained the Southern Station national attention. Blue stain was a major economic problem for lumbermen. Fungi would discolor the sap wood of pine and reduce lumber value. Lindgren found a chemical that when added to water made an effective dip that controlled the problem.

The Southern Forest Survey was another early accomplishment that gained the Southern Station invaluable support. The survey data—the actual survey unit stands, growth, and yield figures—began coming out and the pulp and paper industry used this information to bring new industry to the South.

Demmon transferred from the Southern Station in 1944 to assume the director position in the Lake States Forest Experiment Station. After a number of years there, he became the director of the Southeastern Research Station in Asheville, NC. Demmon was a highly respected forestry research leader. He was elected chair of both the Society of American Foresters and of the American Forestry Association.

References

Demmon, E.L. 1942. Twenty years of forest research in the Lower South, 1921-1941. Journal of Forestry. 40(1): 33-36.

Maunder, E.R. 1977. Voices from the South: recollections of four foresters; Inman F. Eldredge, Elwood L. Demmon, Walter H. Damtoft, Clinton H. Coulter. Santa Cruz, CA: Forest History Society, Inc. 252 p.

U.S. Forest Service. 1929. Volume, yield, and stand tables for second-growth southern pines. Misc. Pub. 50. Washington, DC: U.S. Department of Agriculture, Forest Service. 202 p.

Wakeley, P.C. 1964. A biased history of the Southern Forest Experiment Station through fiscal year 1933. Unpublished document. New Orleans, LA: On file with: USDA Forest Service, Southern Research Station, Forest Management Research, Pineville, LA 71360.

Wakeley, P.C. 1978. The adolescence of forestry research in the South. Journal of Forest History. 22(7): 135-145.

Kisatchie National Forest's Longest Serving Supervisor

HUGH S. REDDING

Hugh Redding served as supervisor for the Kisatchie National Forest (Kisatchie) for more than 12 years, from 1945 to 1957, twice as long as any other supervisor. His other experiences on the Kisatchie included serving as district ranger in 1934 and as assistant supervisor from 1935 to 1945. This period was particularly difficult due to great reforestation need, few employees during World War II, and restructuring the forest after the war. Although Redding was a real character, he was admirably suited for the tasks at hand.

Hugh Redding led the Kisatchie National Forest through the turbulent years of World War II and into the 1950s when the demand for wood products grew rapidly.

Born in North Carolina the son of a "peckerwood" mill owner, he soon moved to Montana and was driving logs down rivers before he was 15 years old. Although he obtained a degree in forest engineering from the University of Montana, he would rather tell you about the days of his experiences in logging camps when he carried his "turkey," or bedding roll, on his back from one logging camp to another. Before he went to college he described himself as an expert in "flatheadin', tie hackin', skiddin', sleigh haulin', chutin', flumin', river drivin', crusin', scalin', and any other doggone thing."

Redding was employed by the Forest Service in 1922 and worked in Washington, Montana, and Idaho, before moving to the Kisatchie National Forest in 1934. While Redding was described as one of the Forest Service's choice products and most enthusiastic adherents to its aims and objectives, he seemed difficult to discipline. He became known as the Forest Service's "Peck's Bad Boy" after a popular newspaper fictional series describing a mischievous lad who loved to play sneaky pranks on others. The "Peck's Bad Boy" tag was a popular term for any incorrigible rule-breaker.

The land purchased for Kisatchie consisted primarily of cutover areas devoid of standing timber. Redding had submitted so many requests for funding for reforestation that his supervisor in Atlanta said that "there couldn't be that much cutover land in Southwest Louisiana as you say." In an opportunity to show the Atlanta supervisor the forest lands, Redding put his point across by planning a route on the Kisatchie so that they did not "see a stick of timber" in 5 hours of travel. At 7 o'clock that night, the visitor exclaimed, "My God, Redding, let me see one tree before I go back to Atlanta?"

Some of his coworkers recalled that "Uncle Hugh" could spend an evening when out of town drinking water glasses full of spirits, but he would always be up the next morning at 6 a.m., whistling and singing, apparently with no ill effects! Redding took his responsibility as administrator of Kisatchie's forests very seriously, firmly believing that forests cannot be separated from people. Hugh was several decades ahead of his time in realizing the importance of input from the public. He stated, "Forests are not a resource that can be enclosed behind a big fence and managed for a single purpose.... Unless the public generally knows and feels that it is participating in the activities which are necessary to make forests productive, they not only refuse to cooperate and assist, but they actually hinder the efforts…, because they were not considered in the formulation of the plans which concerned them at least directly."

The time of Redding's service was a period of transition from the Great Depression through World War II, to peace and the return to civilian life of millions of former servicemen. The reforestation efforts from the 1930s through the 1950s resulted in one of the most productive forests in the South. The leadership of Redding helped prepare the forest for the great demand of wood products that began during the 1960s and 1970s as the economy of the country expanded greatly.

Many who knew Redding would echo the summation voiced by one employee: "Hugh Redding—that was a good guy."

References

Burns, A.C. 1982. The Kisatchie story: a history of Louisiana's only national forest. Lafayette, LA: University of Southwestern Louisiana. Ph D. dissertation.

Kerr, E.; Morgan, E.1995. The people's forest. Forests & People. 5(4): 8-19.

Legendary Ranger of Winn Ranger District

GEORGE M. TANNEHILL, JR.

George M. Tannehill served as the Winn District ranger for 38 years, the longest tenure of any ranger on the Kisatchie National Forest and the second to only one ranger in the entire Forest Service. Tannehill was reared in Urania, LA and was a member of the Tannehill family that was closely connected for many years to the historic Urania Lumber Company. George came from a forestry family and was reared in a forestry community, so it is not surprising that he grew up to be a professional forester.

As a youth, he traveled to California, and in 1929 began to work for the Forest Service. After a few months, he returned to Louisiana and enrolled in Louisiana State University's School of Forestry. Upon graduating in 1932, he returned to work for the Forest Service, accepting a position on Ouachita National Forest. In 1935, he came to Winnfield to accept the position as ranger of the Winn District. Although he was responsible for the timber program, recreation, fire control, and road construction and repair, his biggest challenge was supervising an extensive reforestation program. Today, more than 100,000 district acres have been planted.

It was Tannehill's choice to remain in the Winn District until retirement, although the Forest Service wanted to transfer and promote him many times. He refused to leave the district because he believed that he could do more good on the Winn District than anywhere else. If pushed to transfer, George would call "Cousin Allen," Senator Allen Ellender who was President *pro tem* of the Senate, who could cut through a lot of bureaucracy. George also had a close relationship with Senator Russell Long. These friendships helped protect George's position in an Agency that typically moved employees every few years.

Tannehill had a very good relationship with coworkers and citizens of the community. He was held in great respect for his professionalism—he was among the earliest graduate foresters on the Kisatchie—and his fellow citizens demonstrated love for "Mr. George." The many "Mr. George" stories show the high regard with which he was held. Perhaps the secret of Tannehill's success was that "he treated the lowest man on the job the same as someone from the Supervisor's office."

Friends and colleagues had reason to believe Tannehill was a millionaire and the wealthiest ranger in the Forest Service. If so, this wealth must have come from his family's forestry enterprise. Certainly, he did not flaunt his wealth. In fact, one would never know it from the old automobile he drove. According to one of his supervisors, George gave away "two or three fortunes" because he was a "sucker for a sob story." He kept his charity secret, usually sending help through a third party.

Tannehill believed in taking care of the forest. A colleague remembers him as "different from any other ranger I ever worked for—a business type didn't carry on any foolishness. If he promised something, he'd work hard to try to get it done." Others remember him as always being immaculate. When in civilian clothes, he dressed with shirt and tie, looking as if he had "just stepped out of a band box."

He developed a unique relationship with the public by using unconventional methods. The arson problem common to all districts was reduced on the Winn District when he reduced the number of fires by hiring the woods burners. In those early days it was critical to win over the local citizens who for years had done as they pleased with stock, timber trespass, hunting, and fire on what had become government land.

Tannehill was described as the "type that would not tell you any more than he had to, letting you go your merry way and get yourself into trouble." When two fire inspectors came from the Atlanta office, they thought that Tannehill should keep his fire towers manned at night because the wind had not died down. After dark, they called him from their hotel with an "I-told-you-so" tone, and told him the whole country was burning—they could see the glow in the sky. George drove the men out to Sparta, LA where a gas well flare was burning, lighting up the sky just as it did every night.

Tannehill is remembered fondly by those who worked for him as one of the smartest foresters they ever knew, "a man with a lot of horse sense as well as college sense." He was respected greatly by employees, colleagues, and the general public.

George Tannehill on his horse and well dressed as usual. Tannehill's saddle is still prominently displayed in the Winn Ranger District offices.

References

Anon. 1970. George M. Tannehill. Forests & People. 20(3): 27, 42.

Burns, A.C. 1982. The Kisatchie story: a history of Louisiana's only national forest. Lafayette, LA: University of Southwestern Louisiana. Ph D. dissertation.

Hillman, L.L. 1978. George M. Tannehill Jr. and the Winn Ranger District: a success story on Kisatchie. Forests & People. 28(1): 16-17, 34.

Louisiana Forestry Commission

I focus on the Louisiana Forestry Commission as a State forestry agency because it was one of the earliest in the South and because its leadership is most familiar to me. Many such State agencies have had a tenuous existence early in their establishment. The Louisiana Forestry Commission is no exception. It has had periods of outstanding professional leadership and other periods that were seriously affected by politics.

Although Hans Enghardt did not have significant administrative responsibility, his inclusion in the profiles demonstrates the collaborative nature of the inter-organizational efforts existing after World War II.

Victor Hugo Sonderegger

Victor Hugo Sonderegger, a native of Winnfield, LA and two-time State forester, may have been named for the French playwright who was the champion of the people, but his time in office was more characterized by a man alone at the top. There were accomplishments during the 14 years he served, but it was a reform movement that sounded the end of his career.

Sonderegger graduated in 1911 from the Biltmore Forest School which provided 1 year of practical forestry training. When R.D. Forbes became the State forester of Louisiana in 1918, he hired Sonderegger as his first assistant. Sonderegger had worked for the Mansfield Lumber Company in Winnfield prior to this position. In 1921, when Forbes left to become the first director of the Forest Service's Southern Station, Sonderegger was elevated to State forester. He did not fill the assistant State forester position, and remained the only professionally trained forester in the organization.

As State forester, Sonderegger carried out a number of projects that Forbes had initiated: fire patrols, railroad fire prevention, publicity, and education.

On the firefighting front, Sonderegger divided the State into two areas with a chief ranger in charge of each. Recruitment of patrolmen and fire wardens followed. In 1922 and 1923, two fire towers were constructed. One was on Great Southern's land and the other was at Urania.

His administration was active in proposing forestry legislation. Notable accomplishments were: (1) penalties for setting fire to State land, (2) provision for establishing national forests, (3) acceptance of lands donated for State forests, (4) establishment of Arbor Day in schools, and (5) a comprehensive seed-tree law.

In 1923, 2,200 acres of land from H.S. Burrowes were acquired by Louisiana for a State forest. The area near Lecompte was officially named the M.L. Alexander Memorial State Forest in honor of Alexander who served as Commissioner of Conservation from 1912 to 1923. Additional land was added to the property and today it comprises 8,000 acres.

Funds became available under the Federal Clarke-McNary law to establish a nursery on the State forest site in 1925. Charles and Luther Delaney were in charge of the nursery program. Within 3 years, they were able to grow and distribute more than a million seedlings.

V.H. Sonderegger, a native of Winnfield, LA, served as State forester during two difficult economic times.

Progress was made on the information and education front by appointing Caroline C. Dormon as instructor of forestry in late 1920. She proved during her stay until 1923 to have a genuine love of forestry and did much to establish an education program in schools. She was an outstanding authority on dendrology and became the first woman elected to membership in the Society of American Foresters.

The first regime of Sonderegger ended on October 1, 1925. One of the problems he had faced was keeping competent employees. His management style was not one that resulted in a stable workforce.

But this was not the end of his involvement in State forestry. He was succeeded as State forester by W.R. (Billy) Hine, a graduate of Cornell University, who had worked with the Southern Station. Hine did a remarkable job of improving the fire protection organization, constructing an additional 13 lookout towers, rehiring Caroline Dormon as assistant in public relations, and beginning a training program for employees.

Hine recruited Nathan D. Canterbury as assistant forester in charge of the nursery program. Canterbury received his master of forestry degree in 1922 from Yale and was very capable. He was one of a few students who received a master's degree without first receiving a bachelor's degree. The nursery program expanded rapidly, and Canterbury led the development of other programs.

Nathan Canterbury was Louisiana State forester for a month and a day.

However, politics began to overshadow the developing forestry programs. Huey Long was elected Governor and planned to oust the Commissioner of Conservation and his staff. State forester Hine had an opportunity to take a Forest Service position and resigned before Long became Governor. V.K. Irion, the Commissioner of Conservation, named Canterbury State forester telling him, "it probably won't last long, but at least you can say you were once the State forester." Irion's words were true—Canterbury was in office only a month and a day. However, he moved on to a long and illustrious forestry career.

Huey Long dismissed personnel of the Department of Conservation en masse. Canterbury stayed over a day to orient the new State forester. He was introduced to the familiar V.H. Sonderegger who was from the same hometown as Governor Long. Canterbury stayed long enough to glimpse how new employees were hired. Each new employee came with a slip of paper signed by the new Commissioner of Conservation specifying the amount of salary the employee would receive—no mention of what position the employee would hold.

Over time, Sonderegger would rehire many of the employees that were fired by Long. Also, he continued much of the effort established by previous State forester Billy Hine. Sonderegger remained in office until 1940 when a reform movement called for a modern and complete forestry program.

The Sonderegger name took on a hint of infamy for two notable events. First, the Society of American Foresters removed him from its rolls because of questionable political activities. Then his name was added to a new pine species.

H.H. Chapman described a natural hybrid of loblolly and longleaf pine and named it Sondergger pine (X *Pinus sondereggeri* Chapman). Some believed, knowing Chapman, that it was named more in recognition of the common name, bastard pine, than as an honor. During Sonderegger's two terms as State forester, he did not hire a single professional forester. Apparently, he did not want competition from college-trained foresters.

Sonderegger's second regime faced many challenges as he served during the Depression. He was responsible for establishing 20 Civilian Conservation Corps camps in Louisiana. These camps made remarkable contributions to the State.

Sonderegger served during a difficult time and had no ulterior motives. He had the interest of the organization at heart. Although wrong in strategy at times, he did what he thought was right for forestry.

JAMES E. (JIM) MIXON

He was described as looking like a modern-day West Texas sheriff: tall and slim, cordial and affable with a quick mind—and a black string tie to top it off. His parents had named him James E. Mixon. That name did not really fit, and he was known by all as Jim Mixon. Mixon's father was a Navy man, and Mixon moved to 13 different schools getting an education. He was born in New Orleans, LA and returned to Louisiana to obtain a forestry degree from Louisiana State University in 1936.

Mixon worked for the Civilian Conservation Corps for a year and then was hired by the Florida Forestry Service as a nurseryman. In 1940, Jim was named forest superintendent for the Louisiana Forestry Commission's State forest at Woodworth, LA. Forestry in Louisiana at the time was in doldrums; virgin forests had been cut out and reforestation just started. With the advent of World War II, only four foresters remained in the Agency. Jim was discharged from the U.S. Army because of a medical problem.

Jim Mixon was State forester of Louisiana for 29 years. He was respected by each administration.

Jim Mixon was named State forester by Louisiana's Board of Forestry Commissioners in 1947. This was a positive move since the Governor had previously appointed the State forester. At the time, Louisiana had one of the worst forest fire records in the South. Previous State forester, Massey Anderson had few resources, neither personnel nor equipment, for providing fire protection.

Mixon was to remain State forester for 29 years, outlasting the administrations of seven Governors. Under his leadership the fire problem was reduced to manageable proportions, Forestry Commission nursery seedling production was greatly increased, public education efforts to alert the citizenry to forestry's needs and potential were expanded, and the Forestry Commission became a model State agency.

Achieving what he accomplished required tremendous determination and dedication, Mixon had strong views on fire causes and they became nationally known in the mid-1950s when he dared to name arsonists as the real cause of the South's devastating forest fire problem. Law enforcement was all the arsonists would understand, he believed, and that is what he gave them.

The Forestry Commission acquired new equipment appropriate for fire protection. To improve the public perception of the agency, Mixon established his annual

"100 point inspection." He was a son of a career Navy man and had a spit-and-polish philosophy about equipment maintenance. Every piece of equipment belonging to the Forestry Commission was subjected to an inspection so exacting that one employee fainted at the scene.

Mixon gained widespread respect from how he handled recurring political pressures. The way Mixon worded it, "I promised them whatever they wanted and then did what I wanted." He told the story: "Earl Long called me up one time and said, 'Jim, I'm a little red in the face about something that has happened—you know, one of my relatives on the fire crew in Winn Parish was fired. How am I going to explain this to my kinfolks?' I told him, 'Governor, I was concerned that you would be embarrassed if I didn't fire him. He's a drinking man and I was afraid it would get out that one of the Governor's relatives was drunk and on the State payroll, supposed to put out fires.' Earl thought about it for a minute, then asked me what I thought he ought to do. I said, 'Well, I thought the highway department would be the right place for him.' The Governor thought that was a good idea, and that's where he put the displaced fellow."

Another Governor objected strongly to the string ties that Mixon wore. Mixon would keep a four-in-hand tie in his desk drawer to slip on whenever he was to meet with the chief executive. It did not always match the suit he happened to be wearing, but the Governor never seemed to notice. Mixon was known for his "unaffected and unabashed outspokenness, no-nonsense practicality…and a propensity for string ties."

Jim Kitchen, who served 11 years as information and education chief with the Forestry Commission and moved on to major forest industry responsibility, described Mixon: "He has rendered outstanding service to the forestry interests of Louisiana… by molding a strong professional organization with high *esprit de corps*; he has afforded an excellent administration and supervision; and he has managed to do all of this in complete cooperation with the changing political administrations of public office holders in Louisiana."

HANS ENGHARDT

Shortly after World War II, Hans Enghardt, a German forester from the Black Forest region, arrived in Alexandria to help restore Louisiana's cutover forests. Seems incongruous—but true. This begins an interesting story of cooperation among governments, agencies, and people.

At the end of World War II, millions of acres of Louisiana forest land remained denuded of trees and both State and Federal agencies sought ways to overcome the problem of this reforestation backlog. In addition to developing a functioning State forestry agency to address these management issues, the Louisiana Forestry Commission (now Louisiana Department of Agriculture and Forestry, Office of Forestry) was given an additional mandate to conduct forestry research.

With limited resources, Jim Mixon, newly appointed State forester, sought ways to address these issues. Mixon quickly developed a close friendship with Bill Mann, leader of the Forest Service's Southern Station program in Alexandria, LA. In 1948, a memorandum of understanding between the organizations was approved that provided for collaborative efforts. Initially, Mixon provided funding to support the Southern Station's research program.

However, in 1955, Mixon agreed to sponsor a forester from Germany who would have research responsibility. After the war, the United States agreed to allow immigration of German citizens whose training and skills were needed in the United States. The Department of State approved the immigration of Enghardt and his family under the sponsorship of the Louisiana Forestry Commission.

Since the Forestry Commission had no research organization, Mixon assigned Enghardt to the Southern Station. Enghardt, his wife, small son, and pet dachshund arrived in Alexandria, LA in February 1956. Hans assignment was to develop silvicultural and management recommendations for southern pine plantations.

Under the unique arrangement, Enghardt became an integral part of the Southern Station's research program. However, he was always a State employee. During the next 17 years, Enghardt's expertise contributed significantly to the understanding of pine plantation management. As would be expected from Enghardt's training and nature, he was very meticulous and thorough. He developed an elaborate color coding system to record certain field data, the

Hans Enghardt photo taken in the mid-1960s.

meaning of which was not made clear to his successor, Don Feduccia. This caused considerable consternation.

During WWII, Enghardt had manned an anti-aircraft battery in the German army. During a group discussion of assignments during the war, it became obvious that Enghardt's anti-aircraft battery shot down an American bomber over the Alps flown by Lew Grosenbaugh, a Southern Station assistant director. There was a cordial laugh about the experience, but it seemed to those present that Enghardt was somewhat more pleased about the discussion than Lew.

Hans enrolled in the LSU Graduate School's forestry program to improve his knowledge of southern forestry practices. He was able to meet most of the course requirements by attending LSU-Alexandria. Faculty from LSU's forestry school taught evening courses because there were a number of veterans and others who wanted to obtain graduate degrees while employed by Federal, State, and private forestry organizations. Enghardt graduated with a master's degree in forestry in 1966.

The Enghardt family was incorporated into the local community. Michael, the son, was an excellent student. Upon graduating from high school, Michael joined the U.S. Navy, received his medical school training through a recruitment program, and served as a physician in some of the military's most prestigious medical facilities. He retired from the U.S. Navy in 1997.

After 17 years working for State and Federal government programs in Louisiana, Enghardt became interested in returning to Germany. He applied for admission to the University of Freiberg. In 1973, Enghardt and his wife returned to the university where he had obtained his undergraduate training. He received his doctoral degree and moved back to Baden-Baden, his hometown. Enghardt was hired by Germany's Federal forestry organization and again worked in the Black Forest Mountains, where he became internationally recognized for his work on the effect of acid rain on Black Forest tree species.

Enghardt's career shows the value of developing relationships—both personally, and also between governments, and between Federal, State, and local organizations. Enghardt was wise when he realized his contributions to Louisiana's forestry community had peaked. He, then, accepted the challenge of returning to his native Germany where he trained himself to deal with significant problems in the forests of his home country.

Enghardt retired in Baden-Baden. He touched many lives and provided knowledge to help resolve significant forestry issues. His capacity to adapt to new challenges and meet them positively was a hallmark of his career.

References

Anon. 1963. Sonderegger's regime (1921-1925). Forests & People. 13(1): 25-27.

Anon. 1963. Return of Sonderegger (1929-1940). Forest & People. 13(1): 32-33.

Anon. 1967. An interview with Jim Mixon. Forests & People. 17(2): 24-25, 37.

Anon. 1977. State forester Jim Mixon—one more salute from his friends. Forests & People. 27(1): 40-42.

Barnett, J. 2009. Sonderegger as State forester made quite a name for himself. Forests & People. 59(1): 14-15.

Burns, A.C. 1968. A history of the Louisiana Forestry Commission. Louisiana Studies Institute Monograph Series. Natchitoches, LA: Northwestern State University.

Enghardt, H. 1957. I was a forester in Baden Baden. Forests & People. 7(3): 36-37, 48-49.

Louisiana Forestry Association

The idea to form a group to promote forestry was first developed and organized in Louisiana in 1909. The resulting Louisiana Forestry Association was dissolved in the late 1920s and early 1930s due to membership lapsing when most mills discontinued operation.

During a meeting of the Gulf States Section of the Society of American Foresters in New Orleans, LA in the fall of 1940, a reorganization of the association was discussed. However, it was in 1947 after World War II that action was taken. An effort was undertaken by the North Louisiana Group, headed by Lloyd Blackwell, to form a committee that would guide the development of an association. In the fall of 1947, the committee voted to organize the Louisiana Forestry Association. Lloyd Blackwell was appointed as acting executive secretary for the organization.

J.H. (Jim) Kitchens, Jr.

Born into a sawmill family in Trout, Louisiana, in 1913, James H. Kitchens, Jr. was well oriented in timberlands and sawmilling long before he received his forestry degree from Louisiana State University in 1937. He pursued a law course several years before settling into forestry as a career. When he graduated, jobs were scarce so he worked on a Soil Conservation Service project funded by the Works Projects Administration (WPA) for 18 months. He received an appointment with the Tennessee Valley Authority (TVA) in 1938 and spent the next 2 years engaged in fire prevention activities where he pioneered the art of communicating conservation lore to all levels of society. His interests were always in public relations, rather than traditional forestry.

In 1940, then Louisiana Gov. Sam Jones revitalized the Louisiana Forestry Commission and staffed the organization with professional foresters. Kitchens began his tenure as chief of information and education with the Louisiana Forestry Commission in New Orleans, LA. However, his

Jim Kitchens was an early promoter of forestry practices in Louisiana and the South.

assignment in this capacity was interrupted in 1942 by a tour of duty in the U.S. Army that lasted nearly 4 years. For 11 months of that time, he served in the European Theatre with the 95th Infantry Division. He was awarded three Battle Stars, the Bronze Star, and the Combat Infantry Badge. His army career continued in a reserve capacity until 1957 when he retired as a Major with 23 years of service.

Following World War II, Kitchens returned to the Louisiana Forestry Commission and was located in Baton Rouge, LA. He quickly gained national recognition in forestry education circles because of his leadership in the publication of the textbook "Ten Lessons in Forestry" and the companion teacher manual "Behind the Curtain of Green." He also led the organization of information and education chiefs for all 12 Southern States to coordinate forestry education efforts on a regional scale.

Kitchens became executive director of the Louisiana Forestry Association in 1951 when he replaced John Ferran who had died unexpectedly. He teamed up with the Association's outstanding Editorial Advisory Committee to publish the *Forests & People* magazine. He led the effort for 8 years and during that time the magazine twice was recognized as the best of its kind in the Nation. Always using a positive approach, and working with member-committee groups, Kitchens managed the affairs of the Louisiana Forestry Association through years which saw basic reforms in the forestry environment of Louisiana. These included a modern forest tax law, expanded and improved forest fire protection, a hog control law, and a comprehensive program of forest research. Kitchens was the catalyst, the talent and leadership of the association that was in the forefront of a movement that pushed forestry among the top industries in Louisiana.

Kitchens entered the employment of T.L. James & Company, Inc., in 1959 as assistant director of their Forestry Division. He led the reforestation of over 100,000 acres of cutover forest land and implemented extensive forest management programs of that company. He also paid a major role in inducing capital investments by forest industries and helping create thousands of jobs for his fellow citizens.

Kitchens was a gentleman from the old school—a tall, lanky son of a sawmill man that used his talents to bring forestry into the modern age. Many of the benefits which the forestry community in Louisiana enjoys today are due to the leadership of this man.

CHARLES H. (CHARLIE) LEWIS, JR.

Charles (Charlie) Lewis, Jr., was born in 1916 in Randolph, LA, a sawmill town in Union Parish that disappeared when the sawmill closed. He grew up in Natchez, MS and attended Louisiana State University on a tennis scholarship. He graduated with a degree in forestry in 1939 and began his career as a forester for Crosby Lumber and Manufacturing Company in Crosby, MS. His employment was interrupted by World War II, during which he served in the U.S. Army Air Corps as a fighter pilot. He completed his military service in 1945 with the rank of Major and as a Squadron Commander.

After the war, Lewis returned to the Crosby Lumber Company in the capacity of chief forester for Crosby Chemicals in DeRidder, LA. In 1959, he became executive director of the Louisiana Forestry Association. As executive director, he left an indelible mark on the association and the

Charlie Lewis, a master of public relations and promoter of forestry practices in the South.

growth of forestry in Louisiana. He was a master of public relations and led with a unique style and unflappable attitude. In a time when forestry was just expanding, he gained support for forestry programs with messages that were anything but boring.

Contemporaries remember his presentations well: he could recite the returns on investment in reforestation and punctuate it by throwing seedlings into the audience. He had his own version of a striptease where he would remove all items that were not made from a forest product. In winter visits to congressional delegations in Washington, DC, he would bring boxes of camellias to soften his entry into every office.

These were attention-getters, but the substance of his work was very important. He and the association justified expansion of reforestation programs, pushed for research and development that resulted in the plywood industry in the South, and led the effort to stabilize tax assessments on forest land.

After 7 years with the Louisiana Forestry Association, Lewis began an association with Georgia Pacific in Conroe, TX, where he was instrumental in establishing the regional office of Louisiana Pacific. He was also very involved in professional organizations, including numerous regional and national positions in the Society of American Foresters. He retired from Louisiana Pacific in 1974.

Louis survived three airplane crashes during World War II with minor scratches. Then in 1974, he jumped a 3-foot ditch in Spain during a golf tournament and ruptured five discs in his lower back. He became an invalid for 2 years. Always involved in meaningful avocations such as church leadership positions, tennis, golf, sailing, and wood working, during his recovery he studied hydroponic gardening and developed a greenhouse to grow vegetables that he shared with friends and neighbors. Always involved, Charlie adhered to his motto, "Never Give Up." Louis died in May 2008.

A resolution by the Louisiana Forestry Association reads in part, "Charlie Lewis exemplified the highest moral and ethical standards in all his business and professional activities…, and this spirited and influential gentleman possessed innumerable fine qualities. He shall be remembered by those who know him best for his wisdom, strong convictions, and leadership."

References

Anon. 1963. Formation of the Louisiana Forestry Association. Forests & People. 13(1): 76. 112-119.

Anon. 1966. Faces of forestry: J.H. Kitchens, Jr. Forests & People. 16(3): 33.

Anon. 1997. Executive directors: a hard message to sell. Forests & People. 47(2): 9, 14.

Kerr, E. 1975. A salute to Gentleman Jim. Forests & People. 25(2): 24-25.

Tompkins, J. 1997. Jim Kitchens: true forester as leader. Forests & People. 47(2): 32.

FOREST MANAGEMENT

Once reforestation became successful, many questions arose about how stands should be managed to make forests economically sustainable. Fortunately, a number of remarkable individuals devoted their careers to developing answers to these questions.

The following profiles reflect the contributions of a number of these individuals. Areas of emphasis ranged from uneven-aged and even-aged pine silviculture to management of hardwood forests that had been generally neglected. Supporting these efforts was seed production and direct seeding—a needed approach to reforest cutover stands.

Not to be overlooked is the development of statistical procedures and mensurational (the branch of mathematics dealing with measurements) techniques. This information was critical to understanding and developing technology and applying it to established forests.

Uneven-aged Pine Management
RUSSELL R. (RUSS) REYNOLDS

The Crossett Experimental Forest, located south of Crossett, AR, and just north of the Louisiana State line, was established by the Forest Service, Southern Station in 1933.

It resulted from a cooperative agreement with the Crossett Lumber Company that donated about 1,600 acres to the Station with a provision that the forest could be returned after 20 years.

Russell R. (Russ) Reynolds, a native of Michigan, graduated from the University of Michigan with a B.S. degree and an M.S. degree, and joined the Forest Service, Southern Station in 1930. Reynolds was assigned to the Crossett Experimental Forest when it opened in 1933, and spent the next 34 years establishing and directing the research center.

Early in the development of the Crossett Experimental Forest, it was decided to establish the Crossett Research Center on the forest. This was to become the first Forest Service branch research station in the South. Due to lack of funds for establishment, the buildings for the center and staff housing were constructed with pine logs harvested from the forest.

Reynolds and his wife, Geneva, lived in Crossett at the Rose Inn while housing was constructed on the experimental forest. The Rose Inn was owned by the Crossett Lumber Company and provided the only public housing in the town. The large Rose Inn dining room, always with sparkling white tablecloths, was famous for its good food. For many years, men had to wear ties and coats before they were admitted to the room. However, to assure that no one was turned away, a supply of extra coats and ties was kept outside the room. Lodgers paid $30 per month to live and eat at the hotel.

Russ Reynolds interacting with 4-H students at one of his "Farm Forty Days" on the Crossett Experimental Forest.

Reynolds' research began with the goal of determining how to cut the cutover mixed pine-hardwood forests of Arkansas and north Louisiana at a profit while at the same time maintaining and improving the stand of timber. In 1937, Reynolds established the famous "Poor" and "Good" farm forestry forties. Reynolds and his colleagues evaluated whether previously unmanaged, understocked, second-growth loblolly-shortleaf stands could be successfully rehabilitated and managed using the selection cutting (uneven-aged management) technique.

Meticulous records were kept so that the economics of this management could be evaluated. An important aspect of management was to remove cull hardwoods. Reynolds was fortunate in that the Crossett Lumber Company had a "chemical plant" that used very small hardwood material that was removed from the stands.

Although some criticized Reynolds' success with selection cutting by indicating that the needed intensive competition control efforts were difficult to apply on a large scale and that he had no even-aged management check, Russ's studies did much to convince landowners that forestry was a sound business investment.

His "Farm Forty Days" were an outstanding success. Reynolds used these to demonstrate the large volume of logs, pulpwood, and other products that could be harvested annually from second-growth shortleaf-loblolly pine stands that were managed on the selection system. With great skill, Reynolds converted the poor forty to a good one with profits from the stand each year.

Reynolds spent his career on the Crossett Experimental Forest and earned a number of prestigious awards. In 1947, he received a Superior Service Award for "accomplishments of national significance and value in research on applied forestry management." A similar award was given to him and his staff in 1959 "for exceptional initiative and achievement in developing and disseminating knowledge that stimulated landowners to restore millions of depleted forest acres and then to manage them for profitable timber production."

Truly, Reynolds made a major contribution in the promotion and understanding of forestry to small landowners across the South.

References

Anon. 1968. Faces of forestry—Russ Reynolds. Forests & People. 18(1): 26.

Baker, J.B. 1986. The Crossett farm forestry forties after forty-one years of selection management. Southern Journal of Applied Forestry. 10(10): 233-237.

Kerr, E. 1962. Twenty-five years on a poor farm forty. Forests & People. 12(4): 4-9.

Reynolds, R.R. 1980. The Crossett story: the beginning of forestry in southern Arkansas and northern Louisiana. Gen. Tech. Bull. SO-32. New Orleans: U.S. Department of Agriculture, Forest Service, Southern Forest Experiment Station. 40 p.

Wakeley, P.C. 1964. A biased history of the Southern Forest Experiment Station through fiscal year 1933. Unpublished document. New Orleans, LA: On file with: USDA Forest Service, Southern Research Station, Forest Management Research, Pineville, LA 71360.

Even-aged Pine Silviculture
WILLIAM F. (BILL) MANN, JR.

William F. (Bill) Mann, Jr.'s early years hardly give indication that he would one day be recognized as a leading authority on the regeneration and management of southern pines. For there were relatively few trees in Mann's environment—certainly there were no southern pines.

Mann was born in 1916 in New York City's Bronx borough and reared on Long Island. He had no explanation of why he entered Pennsylvania State University as a forestry major. "I don't recall in the slightest how I happened to get into forestry," he said.

In 1940, Mann came to work for the Southern Station in Oxford, MS, on a flood survey. Mann served in the Navy during World War II on the carrier USS Enterprise. Most of his time was spent in the Pacific and when discharged he returned to the Southern Station in Gulfport, MS. He worked there and in Crossett, AR, before coming to Alexandria, LA, in 1951.

Mann became the leader of the Southern Station's even-aged pine silviculture research unit, which under his leadership gained national recognition. In 1961, the unit received a Unit

Bill Mann led timber management research through a period of major transition.

Superior Service award from the U.S. Department of Agriculture Secretary of Agriculture "for developing successful techniques for direct seeding of southern pines, for controlling noxious hardwoods, and for utilizing and improving southern forest ranges."

Mann obtained a master's degree in forestry from Louisiana State University and wrote about 150 publications, most dealing with reforestation and management of newly established stands of southern pines. He became internationally recognized as the authority on direct seeding of the southern pines. Mann and his colleagues developed the repellent coatings for seeds that made direct seeding feasible. As a result of these efforts, more than 280,000 acres in Louisiana and one and a half million acres throughout the South were reforested. The research made feasible the regeneration of the South's cutover longleaf pine forests through aerial seeding and better seed storage techniques. Mann planned, organized, and directed a long-term program of research that reduced the cost of reforesting the southern pinelands by one half.

Although Mann is largely recognized for his research in artificial regeneration, he conducted research and led a research program that was much greater in scope. The unit program was instrumental in developing techniques for controlling unwanted hardwoods in pine stands. In particular, the tree injection techniques that became the mainstay of controlling undesirable woody competition. Mann's interest also included the management of established pine stands. Studies installed by Mann and his colleagues dealt with planting spacing, timing of initial thinning, and amounts and intervals of thinning. These studies continue to provide essential information for the development of growth and yield models for southern pines and now are the basis for developing an understanding of the effects of global climate change. Since much of the cutover land was used for cattle grazing, range management was another early research emphasis. The unit developed a supplemental feeding program for cattle on cutover ranges in the longleaf pine belt. This program provided for a doubling of calf production with only minor expenditures for feed supplements.

Mann was very active in professional organizations and societies. He was elected Fellow in the Society of American Foresters (SAF), served two terms on the SAF's national governing board, was national chair of the SAF's Forestry Fund, was chair of the Gulf States Section, and was chair of the local SAF Chapter. Accomplishments receiving recognition included a 1964 commendation from the Gulf States Section of SAF, named Forest Conservationist of the Year in Louisiana in 1969, and in 1972 received the Barrington Moore Award from the SAF for "outstanding achievement in biological research contributing to forestry."

Mann's management style was a very authoritative one. He was an excellent organizer, but some employees had difficulty with the type of intensive and demanding supervision that they received.

He helped formulate the programs of the Louisiana Forestry Association and served on many of its committees. Mann and his close personal friends, James H. (Jim) Kitchens, Jr., executive secretary, Louisiana Forestry Association and James E. (Jim) Mixon, State forester, Louisiana Forestry Commission, became a "forestry triumvirate" that had unique ability to shape forestry progress in Louisiana and the surrounding States during the late 1950s and 1960s. Their efforts to develop political as well as professional and lay support resulted in their organizations becoming the leading ones at Federal, State, and forest industry levels. They provided an example in forestry leadership that was truly unique. Through their combined efforts the Southern Station research program at Alexandria, LA blossomed. The multimillion dollar Alexandria Forestry Center was dedicated in 1964, following expansions in development of the Palustris Experimental Forest and in numbers of research personnel.

Mann was immensely proud of the fact that his and his unit's research could be put into practical use "practically before we have it published." He said, "It is very frustrating to do research when no one uses it." Upon his death in January 1980, the Louisiana Forestry Association issued a memorial resolution that said in part, "We share the fond memory of a quiet and dedicated man whose work helped transform the fate of our State and the region."

References

Anon. 1968. Faces of forestry: Bill Mann. Forests & People. 18(1): 24-25.

Anon. 1980. A tribute to a trusted advisor. Forests & People. 30(1): 5.

Direct Seeding

HAROLD J. DERR

Many millions of acres of native forests of the South were devastated during the late 1800s and early 1900s. The harvests were so complete that few seed sources remained for natural stand regeneration. As late as 1955, 1.5 million acres of pine forest land in Louisiana alone remained unproductive. The job was so immense that it was projected that many decades would be required to regenerate the land by planting. New approaches to reforestation were needed.

In 1946, the Southern Station of the Forest Service established a research center in Alexandria, LA. One of the missions of the center was to develop techniques to speed the reforestation of cutover forest land. Planting of nursery-grown seedlings was the established technique, but the scope of the problem dictated that new approaches to speed reforestation be developed, and a concentrated effort began to make direct seeding a reality.

Harold Derr joined the Alexandria location of the Southern Station in 1946 at the end of World War II. Harold had graduated from Iowa State University before entering military service and did graduate work at the University of Washington after the war. He had entered the Army as a Private and retired from the U.S. Army Reserve as a Lt. Colonel in the Medical Corps. His medical experience made it appropriate that he was assigned the task of developing repellents for direct seeding technology.

Harold Derr explaining research results to U.S. Senator Allen Ellender.

The concept for direct seeding was not new. For centuries, foresters throughout the world had been intrigued by the simplicity of starting stands by sowing limited quantities of seed at the right time. But, early attempts clearly showed that seed predation by birds and rodents created a great obstacle.

The research was aimed primarily at finding a practical method of protecting seed from birds, since both resident and migratory species are usually numerous when pine seeds are sown in the fall. Rodents, though a problem, were considered easier to cope with.

Derr led the effort to find chemicals that would protect the seeds from predation. He was assisted by Center Leader William F. Mann, Jr. and the assignment of U.S. Fish & Wildlife ornithologist Brooke Meanley to help evaluate bird responses to chemical treatments. The first breakthrough came in 1953 when anthraquinone was found to be an effective, nontoxic bird repellent. Anthraquinone is used in the manufacture of laxatives, photographic materials,

and dyes and is very safe to use. Later tests demonstrated that thiram, a fungicide commonly used in agriculture, was equally effective in protecting seeds from bird predation.

Longleaf pine seeds were sown in the fall since these seeds germinate soon after they are shed from cones, but are exposed to serious predation by rodents. To provide additional protection a small quantity of Endrin, a commercial insecticide, was added to the repellent coating. The seed treatment combination of thiram and Endrin with a latex sticker to bind the chemicals to the seeds provided excellent protection from both bird and rodent predators.

Direct seeding was widely acclaimed during the 1950s and 1960s. Hundreds of thousands of forest land acres were quickly put back into production using this technology, and many publications documented the development of this technology. This effort, led by Harold Derr, resulted in guidelines for successful direct seeding and was published as the handbook "Direct seeding pines in the South." It was published in 1971 as U.S. Department of Agriculture, Agriculture Handbook 391. This research was a basis of the group being awarded the Secretary of Agriculture's Superior Service Award. Derr had already received the National Civil Service League's Award for Excellence in 1964 for his contributions to southern forestry.

Direct seeding technology was quickly and widely applied because it was easier, faster, and cheaper than hand planting. Seeding was extensive in Louisiana due to the need for large-scale reforestation. The T.L. James Company leased nearly 100,000 acres of cutover land. In 1957, seeding was used to quickly get much of it into commercial forest production.

In about 10 years, Derr and his colleagues developed technology to successfully direct seed southern pines—technology that had eluded foresters for many generations. This greatly hastened the reforestation of cutover pine forests. More than 400,000 acres of unproductive forest land in Louisiana and about 3.5 million acres across the South were regenerated by seeding. Seeding was developed to meet a specific reforestation need—large areas of cutover land. It provided the needed technology to regenerate such land in a prompt and economic manner, and its success in meeting this reforestation need began its demise. Seeding often resulted in stands that were over stocked and it required large quantities of seeds. Because of these limitations, planting is again the accepted technology since it is better adapted to the current need for reforestation.

Although Derr's accomplishments are primarily related to direct seeding, he contributed significantly in other areas of research. He worked to improve nursery production of longleaf pine seedlings, to evaluate the effects of pruning limbs on wood quality, and conducted pioneering research on improving the genetics of longleaf pine.

Harold was a warm and gracious individual held in high respect by his friends and collaborative scientists. His leadership in developing tools to hasten the restoration of southern pine forests has had a lasting impact. Hundreds of thousands of acres of productive pine forests are a living legacy of his contributions to southern forestry.

References

Anon. 1956. Faces of forestry: Brooke Meanley. Forests & People. 6(1): 54.

Derr, H J; Mann, W.F, Jr. 1971. Direct seeding pines in the South. Agric. Handb. 391. U S. Department of Agriculture, Forest Service. 68 p.

Statistics and Mensurational Techniques

Early foresters assigned to the Southern Station to conduct research stressed search, observation, and description as an approach to produce sound results. Statistics and mensurational techniques had not yet been developed. Limitations in the application of replication and controls characterized this early research. Phil Wakeley commented that the arrival of Roy Chapman on a permanent basis in 1929 saved the Station's statistical reputation. The assignment of Lew Grosenbaugh almost two decades later continued to make the Southern Station a leader in this field.

Attached to the Southern Station between these two outstanding mensurationists was Frank Freese. In a period when there were few foresters who had statistical training, Freese provided practical and simple publications that allowed foresters to use statistics in their experimentation.

ROY A. CHAPMAN

Roy Chapman was recruited as a temporary field assistant by the Southern Station in 1926 and given a permanent appointment in 1929. Chapman graduated from the University of Minnesota in 1927 and worked for a while for the Forest Service in the Rockies and Minnesota. Always ready with a good story or amusing comment, when transferred to the Southern Station, it was 40 °F below zero when he left a cruising camp in Minnesota; when he arrived in New Orleans, the temperature was 85 °F. Chapman was quoted as saying he "nearly got up and took off his long underwear right in the dining car."

Chapman was a very independent but a most generously helpful man. He was a statistician and an intensely practical one. Phil Wakeley describes his first 2 ½ years on the staff as a strong and stimulating influence in mensurational techniques, experimental design, and analytical procedures. In 1931, he was detailed to Washington to train under Francis X. Schumacher. The assignment lasted for a full 3 years. During the period, Chapman met and formed a friendship with R.A. (later Sir Ronald) Fisher, the father of modern statistics whose published works related to statistics and experimental design did much to shape Chapman's own later career.

Chapman returned to the Southern Station when a number of new studies and projects were getting underway as a result of President Roosevelt's depression relief financing. By enthusiasm, know-how, and personality, he incorporated sound statistical procedures in this new research. Wakeley states that the Southern Station was one of the foremost in incorporating statistics on such a scale. Chapman was described as the Southern Station's real director for scientific work during this period.

Chapman's influence on forestry research was much broader than for the Southern Station. Publications such as "Sampling Methods in Forestry and Range Management" by F.X. Schumacher and himself did much to bring forestry research into a new era of competence.

Roy Chapman was an early statistician and did much to improve the Southern Forest Experiment Station's research program.

FRANK FREESE

A graduate of Yale University and survivor of the World War II's Battle of the Bulge, Frank Freese was assigned to the Southern Station for several years following the war. He is distinguished by the publication of several short books that unraveled the complexity of statistics. The first, called "A Textbook for Statistical Transients," was meant to teach the basics in a readable and simple style. This text was so popular with those who had little statistical training that he wrote two additional understandable and easy to read publications.

Frank Freese's publications did much to improve study design and analysis. (Photo from John Bell Web site)

These classic publications that made forestry statistics understandable are "Elementary Forest Sampling" and "Elementary Statistical Methods for Foresters." In an era when statistics and experimental design were rarely taught in forestry schools, Freese's books were invaluable to foresters involved in any research activity. Not only did they convey in simple language the nature and use of statistics, they provided examples on how to conduct statistical analyses.

In this time of modern unreadable statistical texts, Freese is fondly remembered by those who used his books. He always had a modesty and genuine respect for people that came through in his writing. His books have been reprinted numerous times and are still available in many university bookstores.

Freese moved on to the Madison, WI, Forest Products Laboratory where he spent the latter part of his career. He never married and refused to have a phone in his house. A different thinker was Frank Freese.

LEWIS R. (LEW) GROSENBAUGH

Lewis R. Grosenbaugh earned a degree from Dartmouth College in 1934 and received a master of forestry degree from Yale University in 1936. He began work with the Forest Service's National Forests in Arkansas. In 1946, he was reassigned to the Southern Station in New Orleans, LA where he served as a silviculturist, mensurationist, and finally from 1951 to 1960 as chief of the Division of Forest Management Research.

While with the Southern Station, Grosenbaugh received the Superior Service Award of the U.S. Department of Agriculture. The award was given in 1959 in recognition of his notable contributions in forest management and mensuration, and for excellent leadership in the conduct of forest management research.

Three of his major accomplishments were: (1) developing the point-sampling technique for measuring timber stands, which eliminates the need for laboriously measuring and marking plot boundaries; (2) publishing a revolutionary concept of determining volumes of standing trees by measuring the length of the bole between changes in diameter; and (3) devising a system of sample tree measurement, which can multiply the efficiency of field foresters on such work threefold.

Grosenbaugh was so brilliant that most foresters had difficulty in understanding his new technology. A common joke at forestry group meetings was "you cannot understand his forestry ideas until he has three beers."

Les Grosenbaugh was a very creative scientist and did much to simplify stand measurements.

At a presentation in Grosenbaugh's honor in 1954, Philip A Briegleb, President of the Society of American Foresters, spoke of Grosenbaugh saying that "...his creative contributions to forest management are in daily use throughout the profession. The prestige of American forestry, at home and aboard, has been heightened by his accomplishments. In forest mensuration it would be difficult to name an individual whose work has had greater impact."

In 1961, Grosenbaugh was transferred to the Pacific Southwest Forest and Range Experiment Station in Berkeley to head the Forest Service's first pioneering unit in mensuration. The unit was moved to Atlanta, GA in 1968. Grosenbaugh retired in 1974 as chief mensurationist. Upon his retirement he moved to Gainesville, FL, where he became an adjunct professor of the University of Florida's School of Forest Resources and Conservation.

Grosenbaugh received awards too numerous to mention. One of his supervisors, Charles A. Connaughton who was regional forester of Pacific Southwest and Southern Regions, said of Grosenbaugh: "Along with Lew's ability to 'think ahead,' he has almost limitless mental and physical energy. I'm concerned at times because Lew is spoken of only as a mensurationist. He's a well-rounded forester in field and office skills alike. In addition to the outstanding traits which I've described without many superlatives which are justified, Lew is a 'regular' fellow. He's liked by his associates and his company is sought after when the day is done and relaxation takes the place of business."

References

Anon. 1959. Forests and People salutes Lew Grosenbaugh. Forests & People. 9(3): 21.

Bell, J. 1998. It's the people...Frank Freese. http://www.proaxis. com/~johnbell/itp/itpfreese.htm. [Date accessed: August 11, 2008].

Bell, J. 1995. It's the people...Lewis R. Grosenbaugh. http://www.proaxis. com/~johnbell/itp/itpgros.htm [Date accessed: August 11, 2008].

Burkhart, H.E. Remembering Walter Bitterlich. Journal of Forestry. 106(2): 61.

Freese, F. 1956. A guidebook for statistical transients. New Orleans: U.S. Department of Agriculture, Forest Service, Southern Forest Experiment Station. 77 p.

Freese, F. 1967. Elementary statistical methods for foresters. Agric. Handb. 317. Washington, DC: U.S. Department of Agriculture, Forest Service, Forest Product Laboratory. 87 p.

Freese, F. 1962. Elementary forest sampling. Agric. Handb. 232. Washington, DC: U.S. Department of Agriculture, Forest Service, Southern Forest Experiment Station. 91 p.

Grosenbaugh, L R. 1952. Plotless timber estimates—new, fast, easy. Journal of Forestry. 50: 32-37.

Schumacher, F.X.; Chapman, R.A. 1942. Sampling methods in forestry and range management. Bulletin 7. Durham, NC: School of Forestry, Duke University. 213 p.

Wakeley, P.C. 1964. A biased history of the Southern Forest Experiment Station through fiscal year 1933. Unpublished document. New Orleans, LA: On file with: USDA Forest Service, Southern Research Station, Forest Management Research, Pineville, LA 71360.

Control of Upland Hardwoods

Fred A. Peevy

Much of the South's cutover pine forest land developed scrub stands of low-grade hardwoods that impeded pine reforestation efforts. It became obvious that this hardwood material needed to be removed if productivity of new pine forests was to be optimized.

In 1945, Fred A. Peevy was recruited by the Southern Station and assigned the task of conducting research on cutover pinelands of the South. His initial assignments were to develop better forage for livestock grazing in the cutover land and to find methods of killing undesirable trees and shrubs. Scrub hardwood growth was the exception to the common saying, "One can stand in Central Louisiana and see nothing but tree stumps all the way to Texas."

Peevy graduated from Louisiana State University and when hired by the Forest Service he was working for the Louisiana Agricultural Experiment Station in Baton Rouge, LA. He was transferred to Alexandria, LA in 1946 and became the first professional employee assigned to the Southern Station's Alexandria Research Center.

Although Peevy's initial assignment involved forage research for livestock, he quickly was occupied full time with controlling low-quality woody plants. His was the pioneering effort to develop methodologies to reduce woody plant competition on sites being reforested to pines. His early research provided guidelines for the control of this material; he installed hundreds of studies to evaluate chemicals and application techniques. Early developments included the "hack and squirt" approach. This involved using an axe to cut

Fred Peevy was a pioneer in the development of herbicides and application techniques for controlling competing low-quality hardwoods.

openings in tree stems and squirt a chemical such as Ammate into the cuts or hacks.

These early efforts were hazardous to apply and chemicals lacked much effectiveness. Peevy worked with chemical companies to evaluate new products. Gradually, his research led to effective products and means of application. One of the widely accepted methods involved use of the tree injector. The tree injector consisted of a steel pipe with a cutting blade on one end. The other end had an opening to allow filling with a chemical. Within the blade was an opening through which the chemical was released when the blade was jabbed into a tree. Chemicals such as 2,4-D and 2,4,5-T were commonly used with the approach. Use of the injector was very labor intensive. Injections had to be made continuously around the tree stem. Maintaining crews to apply this technology was difficult—most workers soon realized that there had to be an easier way of making money.

Peevy continued working with new chemicals and found that some could be sprayed on small trees and scrub with good success. Also, certain chemicals could be applied to the soil and would kill hardwood species without hurting pines. Others picked up his developments and continued to refine them. But, Peevy pioneered control of undesirable and cull woody plants. By the end of his career, chemical control of undesirable woody plants was highly effective and widely applied across the South. His work facilitated the reforestation of pine forests across the South.

In recognition of his research, Peevy was part of a team that was awarded the Secretary of Agriculture's Award for Superior Service "for developing successful techniques to regenerate southern pines and for controlling undesirable woody plants." Fred's research was critical to the reforestation efforts that changed the face of the South. He was a kind and gentle individual who will be long remembered by those who had the privilege of knowing him.

References

Peevy, F.A.; Campbell, R.S. 1948. Poisoning southern upland weed trees. Journal of Forestry. 47(6): 443-447.

Peevy, F.A. 1953. Fertilizing and seeding forage on forest range in Louisiana. Agronomy Journal. 45: 164-166.

Peevy, F.A.; Brady, H.A. 1868. Mist blowing versus other methods of foliar sprayers for hardwood control. Weed Science. 16(4): 425-428.

Tree injector for injecting herbicides into undesirable woody plants. Commonly used throughout the South for decades.

Hardwood Management

John A. (Put) Putnam

John (Put) Putnam was born in Michigan, raised in Iowa, and went to school at the University of Michigan. He began work with the Southern Station in New Orleans, LA in 1928 as a field assistant on a bottomland hardwoods reconnaissance. He came with unique and valuable experience acquired in logging hardwood tracts owned by his family. He received a permanent appointment in 1931.

Although established in 1921, the Southern Station did not allow any funds to be spent on bottomland hardwoods. It was not until 1927 that some funds were allocated to survey Delta hardwood resources. The Louisiana Department of Forestry contributed some $5,000 for a survey of the Delta's hardwood resources, conditions, and utilization in the State. G.H. Lentz and John Putnam began the survey in the spring of 1928. Lentz, a recent graduate from the New York State College of Forestry at Syracuse, was an intensely practical man, bursting with energy and self confidence. Putnam was a hardwood enthusiast and even in 1928, probably knew the bottomland types better than any other professional forester in the South. They were an excellent team to undertake this survey.

Lentz's and Putnam's report on the hardwood survey along with some other information was published in 1932 as "The trees of the bottomlands of the Mississippi River Delta Region." This publication won the admiration of a wide and varied audience. Certain master copies were beautifully illustrated with photographs. It was republished by the Station as Occasional Paper No. 27 and began the noted Occasional Paper publication series. Although numbered 27, it was the first issue of the Occasional Paper series—even then, the field of public relations was understood. The Hardwood Survey of 1928 led to the establishment of the Southern Station's bottomland hardwood research center at Stoneville, MS.

In an effort to relocate some cypress plots that had been established in 1914, Lentz and Putnam were led by a local character named Captain Forgery of the Jeanerette Lumber Company into a swamp area in south Louisiana's St. Martin Parish. The water was high in the bottoms; for quite a bit of the way, it was waist deep to Lentz, which meant it was nearly arm-pit deep on Putnam. Forgery who knew the ground well and was fairly sure where the plots lay, said, "You gennlemen come over thisaway. There's a high, dry ridge that'll take us right to the place, and it'll be easier going." They followed and the going was easier, wading up to their knees. Putnam finally asked: "Where's that high, dry ridge you were going to take us to?" The answer was: "Why, Mister, you're on it right now!"

Not until the early 1950s did the economic value of Putnam's work begin to be recognized. Putnam and his colleagues demonstrated on the Delta Experimental Forest at Stoneville, MS that depleted hardwood stands could make a quick comeback if they are supplied with fire protection and a minimum of management. After 1951, more than 40 companies added foresters to their staffs to carry out the management programs recommended by Putnam and his staff.

Near the end of his career, Putnam was awarded for his exceptional service. Director Philip Briegleb of the Southern Station commended Putnam "for exceptional service in determining and demonstrating the opportunities for profit in growing hardwoods, thereby stimulating the management of hardwood forests on private and public lands throughout the South."

Putnam was continuously associated with hardwood forestry for more than 36 years. Millions of acres of public and private hardwood land are now managed according to his recommendations. It is appropriate that he became known as "Mr. Hardwoods."

References

Kerr, E. 1958. History of forestry in Louisiana. Baton Rouge, LA: Louisiana Forestry Commission. 55 p.

Wakeley, P.C. 1964. A biased history of the Southern Forest Experiment Station through fiscal year 1933. Unpublished document. New Orleans, LA: On file with: USDA Forest Service, Southern Research Station, Forest Management Research, Pineville, LA 71360.

John Putnam, expert on southern bottomland hardwoods, became known as "Mr. Hardwoods."

Forest Seed Production

HOWELL C. COBB

With the rapidly increasing use of artificial regeneration to reforest vast acreages of cutover land in the early 1950s, availability of seeds became a limiting factor. Howell Cobb, a forester with the Louisiana Forestry Commission, saw an opportunity to address this need and organized the American Forest Seed Company, Inc. of Alexandria, LA.

Cobb, a native of Lutcher, LA, obtained a degree in forestry from Louisiana State University in 1937. Prior to World War II, he worked for short periods on land acquisition and appraisals for Masonite Corporation, administering farm loans for muskrat trappers for the U.S. Department of Agriculture, and making forest product surveys for American Creosoting Company.

Howell Cobb, developer of modern tree seed processing technology. (Photo from Derwood Delaney)

Cobb entered the U.S. Navy in 1942, was commissioned an officer, and served with amphibious forces in the Pacific. He was assigned as a training officer afloat in Maryland and then returned to the western Pacific before his discharge in 1946. He twice won the Silver Star while serving as commanding officer of landing craft in combat operations.

Upon his release from the Navy, Cobb became chief and first forester for a 500,000-acre tract owned by Southwestern Settlement and Development Corporation (later Temple-Inland Forest Products) of Jasper, TX. In 1950, he returned to Louisiana as district forester for Louisiana Forestry Commission in Natchitoches.

In 1956, Cobb saw the potential of providing pine seeds for the growing planting and direct seeding programs and organized the American Forest Seed Company. The primary species of interest was longleaf pine; at the time its seeds could not be successfully stored from one year to another. The traditional means of processing cones and seeds was to place the cones on racks in barns or warehouses, turn heaters on, and try to circulate hot air through the area. The method could take as much as 3 months to open cones.

Cobb's idea was to provide a quicker and more effective method of opening cones and extracting seeds. He decided to adapt and modify the process used on hybrid seed corn to longleaf pine cones. Basically, the process involved placing cones on racks in compartments in a closed building, forcing air heated to 105 °F into one end, controlling air movement through all racks, and letting the cooled air exit at the other end.

This process resulted in seed extracting in about 3 days and allowed quantities of cones processed to expand dramatically. Once the method was demonstrated to work with longleaf pine seeds, other species were quickly adapted to the process since they are less difficult to process successfully. This process provided the capacity to support developing direct seeding technology that speeded reforestation of southern pine forests.

As Cobb began his business, he hired L. Derwood Delaney, Jr., a recent graduate of Louisiana State University, to become his plant manager. Derwood's father, Luther Delaney, was the first State nurseryman in the South, beginning Louisiana's nursery program in 1925.

Derwood Delaney, President of the Louisiana Forest Seed Company in Woodworth. (Photo from Derwood Delaney)

The American Forest Seed Company was a definite success and expanded with new plants to meet the needs of developing reforestation programs. With Howell Cobb's untimely death in the early 1970s, the company's ownership changed a couple of times. However, Derwood Delaney remained as the plant manager throughout this process. In 1983, Derwood formed the Louisiana Forest Seed Company.

The Louisiana Forest Seed Company became a Delaney family business with two sons involved. This has allowed the company to expand its services by collecting, processing, and storing over 200 species of tree and shrub seeds in addition to the southern pines. The company is now the premier provider of forest seeds in the nation and supplies seeds of many species to a number of other countries.

Cobb's idea of improving quality and expanding production of southern pine seeds has come a long way with the help of his plant manager, Derwood Delaney. Louisiana Forest Seed Company now sets the standard for efficiency of production and seed quality.

References

Anon. 1958. A new industry is born. Forests & People. 8(3): 32-33.

Anon. 1966. The faces of forestry: Howell C. Cobb. Forests & People. 16(2): 24-25.

Camp, P. 1972. Cobb's cone kiln—an international business. Forests & People. 22(1): 14-16, 36.

Consulting Forestry

The use of consultants in forestry is nearly as historic as the practice of forestry itself—certainly this is the case in the South. Once early foresters convinced landowners that there was an economic future in practicing forestry, many needed to hire professional expertise. Two of the individuals who worked across the South were Austin Cary and I.F. (Cap) Eldredge (see earlier profiles). Both had gained recognition in their positions, and when they retired they were asked to assist landowners in developing forest management plans.

They became recognized for their expertise in different areas of forestry. Cary was a promoter of the practice of forest management and the economic potential of cutover forest lands. On the other hand, Eldredge, through his leadership of the first forest survey, understood where sufficient forest resources were present to establish successful processing facilities. This dichotomy in landowner needs continues today.

The following two individuals contributed significantly in developing programs of consulting forestry that are particularly noteworthy.

LESLIE K. (LES) POMEROY

Leslie Pomeroy was born in Hub City, WI, in 1896. He entered the University of Wisconsin to study civil engineering and worked part time in timber testing at the U.S. Forest Products Laboratory with a fellow student, Eugene P. Conner. Pomeroy and his friend Conner dropped out of school to enlist in the armed services during the onset of World War I. Neither was accepted due to physical problems. They returned to the Forest Products Laboratory and engaged in research devoted to kiln drying of timber products. Conner finished his engineering degree, but Pomeroy did not.

After the war ended in 1918, Pomeroy conceived the idea of making a trip around the world to study forestry and related matters in foreign lands. With letters of introduction, Pomeroy and Conner departed in 1919, bound for Japan. They managed to find work doing dry kiln consulting and worked as seamen on an adventure that took them to Japan, Philippines, China, Egypt, India, Siberia, and Italy. They then went across Europe to do forestry research in France and England.

Pomeroy and Conner returned to the United States and were offered jobs by Edward J. Young, president of three southern lumber companies. They were sent to learn to cruise timber and other tasks related to the manufacture of lumber. After 2 years of training, they were given administrative jobs. During a sales trip, Pomeroy called on Herman Kessler, the owner of the Stoughton Wagon Company, maker of wagon wheels. He wanted to sell a small Arkansas sawmill in Wilmar, AR.

In 1925, Pomeroy and Conner moved to Arkansas to become owners of the abandoned sawmill in the ghost town of Wilmar that had neither electricity nor running water. They started Ozark Badger Lumber Company which

Early photo of Les Pomeroy, a premier forestry consultant. (Photo from Mike Pomeroy)

included 160 acres of cutover timberland. At the time, lumber companies had clearcut and hauled timber out by railroad and moved away. These cutover tracts had scant timber left to cut. By selectively marking a few trees per acre to cut, the land became productive enough for Pomeroy and Conner to allow periodic timber cutting while the forest regenerated.

Pomeroy began timber management by surveying the land into 40-acre parcels, cruising the standing timber, establishing the number of board feet per acre, and formulating a cutting plan to be carried out on 5-year rotations. Thus, he became the "father of sustained yield." His management plan was so impressive that H.H. Chapman and Yale University forestry students who came to Hardtner's nearby Urania Lumber Company each year studied his methods. The Ozark Badger Lumber Company now owned a number of small tracts of timber. They became the first to use trucks rather than trains to move timber to the mill.

In the late 1930s, Pomeroy was asked to evaluate the W.T. Smith Lumber Company of Chapman, AL, to survey their situation. The owner, J. Greeley McGowin, a successful lumberman and owner of 190,000 acres of timberland recognized that they were approaching the end of their timber supply. Shortly before his death, he told his sons to give up the mill and organize a wholesale lumber business. However, after his death his sons called upon Pomeroy for his recommendations.

Pomeroy recommended: "If you will acquire 10,000 acres of adjoining timberland, let me divide it into ten operating units, and buy some logs for the next 3 years, you can soon be on a permanent 10-year operating cycle, dividing this 200,000 acres of land into 10 cutting units each of which you will log every 10 years. After you get through, you start around again. You'll have timber forever." This was contrary to prevailing thought, but with open minds they followed his recommendations. The McGowins became the first large-scale operators in the South to put that sustained-yield principle into effect.

So successful was this collaboration that in 1938, Pomeroy joined forces with Julian F. McGowin to form Pomeroy and McGowin Consulting Foresters based in Monticello, AR. During the next 50 years, the company served as consultants to owners of more than 50 million timbered acres in all Southern States and several foreign countries. One of Pomeroy's significant achievements, with the aid of McGowin and Jim Girard of the Forest Service, was the development of volume tables for measuring standing timber.

Pomeroy died in 1976, but the company continues as Larson and McGowin, Inc. headed by L. Keville Larson. Larson comes from the same tradition of talented lumbermen and professional foresters. His mother was Estelle, from the McGowin family, and sister of Julian, Earl, Floyd, and Nick McGowin. The continued success of this consulting group is influenced by the quality of early employees such as: Don Harper, Zeb White, Bill and Ed Gandy, Roy Morgan, Robie Scott, John Wood, Don Sampson, and of course, Julian McGowin.

ZEBULON W. (ZEB) WHITE

Zebulon (Zeb) White was born in Baltimore, MD, in 1915, but grew up in New London, CT where he attended the Buckley School. He graduated from Dartmouth College and later served on the Dartmouth Alumni Council. White then attended Yale University School of Forestry. Graduating in 1938, he got his first job with the Works Project Administration's forest survey in Ohio. What he described as his first "real job" was working as a compass man with Pomeroy and McGowin Consulting Foresters firm in Monticello, AR.

His career in 1940 began with a salary of $3.50 a day plus expenses, which he was very glad to get. During the following 18 years with Pomeroy and McGowin, he was involved in every phase of the operation, including partnership in the firm. "I've cruised every pine county west of the Georgia line," he boasted.

In 1958, he was invited to be Professor of Industrial Forestry at Yale University School of Forestry. He was named Clifton R. Musser Professor in 1961 and became associate dean and director of profession studies in 1965. One responsibility was to organize seminars for middle management workers in forest products industries and southern forest management fieldwork for students each spring.

Zeb White, an outstanding educator and consulting forester.

White took up consulting again in the South again in 1972 when he established his own firm in Hammond, LA. In this position, he worked for every pulp and paper company in this region, as well as most lumber companies. His professional expertise included designing inventory studies, conducting resource studies for new plants, and even serving as an executive head hunter. He retired from his consulting firm in 1990, but continued both professional and community involvement.

In what he called his fourth career, White became vice-president of EAI Resource Investments, Inc. which served as a consulting firm that invested pension funds for the Equitable Life Insurance Society Timberfund. In this position, White said, "I'm using my experience to good advantage. I most like going to large tracts and evaluating the timber and investment opportunities for non-forestry people and knowing I'm judging correctly."

Throughout his career, White maintained many professional, civic, and community affiliations and directorships. An Eagle Scout as a youth, he served as scoutmaster both in Monticello, AR, and Woodbridge, CT. A member of Rotary International for most of his career, he was also a literacy volunteer, management consultant, and tutor in southeastern Louisiana. He was elected Fellow of the Society of American Foresters. White felt a commitment to his community regardless of where he lived.

White died in 2001. According to him, he had an ordered life, one full of "White luck" that brought him to his position in life. He made significant contributions to the forestry profession, particularly in the South where he spent much of his career. Always a fun-loving person, he influenced many both within and outside his profession.

References

Anon. 1986. Faces of forestry: a good case of White luck. Forests & People. 36(1): 26-27.

Camp, M. 2008. Leslie Klett (Les) Pomeroy (1896-1976). The encyclopedia of Arkansas history and culture. http://www.encyclopediaofarkansas net/ encyclopedia. Date accessed: December 8, 2008].

Lubell, S.; Pollard, A. 1939. Pine tree bankers. American Forests. 44: 594-596.

McGowin, J F. 1938. The lumberman's viewpoint on the forestry program for the South. Journal of Forestry. 36(6): 572-575.

Walsh, C S. 1994. Member profile: L. Keville Larson, first among his peers. The Consultant. 39(4): 33-35.

EDUCATION

Although the Nation's first forestry school was established in North Carolina at the Vanderbilt Estate, it lasted only 15 years, and it provided practical training in forestry. Foresters who were needed to develop forestry in the South came largely from northern universities. In the early 1900s, forestry schools were established at Yale, Cornell, Michigan, and Minnesota Universities. The earliest forestry school in the South was established at the University of Georgia in 1906. Graduates from all these universities provided leadership and expertise in developing forestry practices throughout the South. Other forestry programs followed quickly. However, graduates from the University of Michigan were frequently heard to tout their number and prominence in southern forestry.

Some of the individuals who were important in bringing forest education to the South are discussed in the following profiles.

Biltmore Forest School
CARL A. SCHENCK

Carl A. Schenck was hired by George Vanderbilt to restore and manage the degraded forests and soils on his large Biltmore Estate near Asheville, NC. Schenck was born in Germany and graduated in 1894 with a Ph.D. degree in forestry. In addition to managing the estate's forest lands, Schenck established the Biltmore Forest School in 1898. He served as the school's director and teacher until the school closed in 1913. Schenck was the first scientifically trained forester employed in the United States, and the Biltmore Forest School is considered the Nation's first forestry school. Cornell University's 4-year forestry program was established a short time later.

Dr. Carl A. Schenck (left) with Henry Hardtner during Schenck's visit to the Urania Lumber Company.

The Biltmore Forest School exposed its students to not only classroom lectures but also practical work experience in the outdoor laboratory of the 120,000 acre Pisgah Forest. Students were instructed in a field-based course of study that included "hands-on" learning. Students devoted an intensive 12 months to forestry in the field, first on a site at the Biltmore Estate, later in active logging areas across the United States and Europe. Following course work, Schenck's "Biltmore boys" were allowed to graduate only after completing an internship on the Biltmore Estate or elsewhere in the timber industry. One of the school's alumni was V.L. Sonderegger who served as Louisiana's State forester in two different administrations.

The school's students initially were sons of wealthy lumber and timber barons, but over the 15 years of the school's existence nearly 400 forestry students were introduced to scientific forestry methods throughout North America. By the time the school closed in 1913, it had produced more than 70 percent of all forestry graduates in the Nation. Schenck's school provided momentum for established universities such as Cornell, Minnesota, and Yale to develop forestry schools of their own.

Graduates of the school described Dr. Schenck as autocratic. He had been raised in a military atmosphere in Germany and did not get along well with the independent mountain folks on the estate. His discipline was pretty harsh, but the students liked him because he was fair. Schenck was tall, slender, and with a large mustache and wore a uniform from one of the German forest services he had been in before coming to the United States. He owned two horses and always rode at full gallop. In fact, students were required to have a horse to ride for their practical training.

Schenck was held in high esteem by his students. He was an excellent teacher and developed a close relationship with the students—they worked together 6 days a week. The students were considered a lusty group, and their exploits in the local bars were loud and long. After repeatedly bailing out students who were thrown in jail, Schenck started Sanger fests—singing and drinking sessions. His thought was "if you're going to do your drinking, let's all do it together." Schenck would provide two kegs of beer and they would sing the school's alma mater, "Down under the Hill," and other drinking songs in school spaces. The words to "Down under the Hill" were written by Douglas S. Rodman, a student in 1902:

> *Down under the hill there is a little still,*
> *And the smoke goes curling to the sky,*
> *You can easily tell by the sniffle and smell,*
> *There's good liquor in the air close by,*
> *For it fills the air with a perfume so rare;*
> *That's only known to a few,*
> *So wrinkle up your lip and take a little sip,*
> *Of good old mountain dew.*

The Biltmore Forest School closed in 1913 due to declining interest in the program and to Schenck's quick temper that resulted in conflict with George Vanderbilt. However, Schenck's influence continued to shape forestry in America.

Schenck retained his German citizenship and was recalled in 1914 to serve as an officer in the German army on the Russian front during WWI. He returned to forestry after the war and traveled in the United States and Europe promoting forest management. He was forced to return to his home again in 1939 with the onslaught of WWII. He resumed his work in the 1940s and was appointed by the U.S. military government as chief forester of the German State of Hesse.

In 1968, the U.S. Congress established the Cradle of Forestry in America National Historic Site to commemorate the Biltmore Forest School. At the site, rehabilitated and reconstructed buildings form part of a living history exhibit dedicated to the school and its programs.

Schenck was one for the foremost pioneers of forestry in the United States and Europe. At the end of his farewell message to the graduates of the Biltmore Forest School, he would always conclude with "Good bye! God bless you, and the United States, and all the workers in her forests."

References

Maunder, E.R. 1977. Voices from the South: recollections of four foresters; Inman F. Eldredge, Elwood L. Demmon, Walter H. Damtoft, Clinton H. Coulter. Santa Cruz, CA: Forest History Society, Inc. 252 p.

Teacher, Artist, Conservationist, and "Mother of the Kisatchie National Forest"

Caroline C. Dormon

In the 1910s, Caroline Dormon experienced the joy of walking though the magnificent old-growth pine forests in the rolling Kisatchie Hills of northern Louisiana. Her father, a small-town lawyer in Arcadia, LA owned a tract of old-growth longleaf pine timber which the family called Briarwood. This timber and the surrounding forests were the inspiration for the love of mature trees and native flora that shaped her life. Saving and preserving them became her obsession.

Seeing the rapid harvest of the old-growth pine forests, Dormon became determined to save some of these forests. She had graduated from Judson College, in Alabama, returned to Louisiana to teach school, and then returned to her Briarwood home near Saline, LA. Her dream was to preserve an area of virgin pine and establish a national forest in the Kisatchie Hills. She and her sister traveled throughout central Louisiana in a Model T Ford identifying areas to suggest as a future national forest.

Caroline Dormon was noted for her expertise with a wide group of native plants as well as her forestry education efforts.

When Dormon read there was to be a Southern Forestry Congress held in New Orleans in 1918, she attended and proposed preservation of some of the virgin forests. Soon afterward, Dormon attended a forestry meeting in Jackson, MS, where she met and discussed her concerns with Col. William B. Greeley, Chief of the Forest Service. Greeley sent W.W. Ashe to meet Dormon in Natchitoches.

Ashe and other Forest Service foresters met with Dormon and traveled on several occasions through the vast area included in the Kisatchie Hills, but Louisiana did not have an Enabling Act that would allow the government to purchase land in the State. Dormon became frustrated with the lack of progress because more and more of the old-growth timber was being harvested.

With the help of her lawyer brother, she wrote an Enabling Act. This she sent to Henry Hardtner, then State Senator, who included it in a forestry bill he was presenting. It passed and become law. In 1928, the first unit of the Kisatchie National Forest was purchased. One of her great regrets was that most of the virgin timber was harvested before the Kisatchie National Forest could be created.

Meanwhile, Dormon became acquainted with Mrs. A.F. Storm, President of the Louisiana Federation of Women's Clubs, and served as her State chair of conservation. Dormon gave countless lectures to clubs, schools, churches, Scouts, and other youth and adult groups. In 1921, she was appointed by M.L. Alexander, Commissioner of Conservation, to handle publicity of that department.

Dormon then accepted a position as chair of publicity and education with the Forestry Division in 1927. In this role she prepared Arbor Day programs, wrote tree books, conducted teacher workshops, prepared bulletins and art work, and established long-lasting programs in conservation across the State.

Because of her significant contribution to forestry, Dormon was the first woman to be elected associate member of the Society of American Foresters. In a letter urging her acceptance by this organization, W.W. Ashe stated: "Miss Dormon was the first and most persistent worker for National Forests in Louisiana...Without question, her efforts have helped shape Louisiana opinion on this policy." She has been called the "Mother of the Kisatchie National Forest" because of these unique contributions.

Although her efforts in the forestry area were notable, Dormon distinguished herself in many other areas. A favorite activity was testing, propagating, and hybridizing plants, particularly the native Louisiana iris. Her plant paintings have been described as "scientifically accurate and incredible in detail." These have been exhibited in numerous art galleries and museums.

She is the author of several books; the most notable is "Wild Flowers of Louisiana," now a collector's item. Six other major publications deal mostly with native iris species. She received four medals from the American Iris Society for developing outstanding hybrids of Louisiana irises. In 1965, in recognition of her lifetime achievements, Louisiana State University conferred on her an honorary doctor of science degree.

Shortly before her death, friends suggested that she will her Briarwood estate to a foundation that would become a center for educational purposes in conservation. Today Briarwood, near Saline, is a nature preserve honoring Dormon's remarkable contributions to conservation. Now, it is open to visitors on weekends in the summertime.

References

Anon. 1963. Caroline Dormon, queen of a forest kingdom. Forests & People. 13(1): 36.

Crittenden, B. 1980. Miss Caroline's dream became Louisiana's national forest. Forests & People. 30(3): 25-26, 28-29.

Johnson, F.H. 1990. The gift of the wild things: the life of Caroline Dormon. Lafayette, LA: University of Southwestern Louisiana Press. 166 p.

Robinson, V.E. 1966. Miss Caroline, Prima Donna of the plant world. Forests & People. 16(3): 30-31.

Yale University Forestry Training at Urania

H.H. (CHAPPY) CHAPMAN

H.H. (Herman Haupt) (Chappy) Chapman was a long-time faculty member of Yale University's School of Forestry who made significant contributions to understanding the practices needed to restore the South's longleaf pine ecosystem. Chapman graduated from the University of Minnesota in the early 1900s. He established a research plantation with red, white, jack, and Scotch pines at the University's experimental farm in 1900—probably the oldest in the Nation. According to his colleagues at Yale, Chapman originally trained as a poultry scientist and was so boisterous about it that he became known as "Chicken Chapman." Described variously as dynamic, dogmatic, charismatic, and impressive and intimidating by students and colleagues, he was known as "Chappy" to his friends. His strong personality had a lasting impact on his students.

Chapman began leading Yale's summer forestry students into the South early in the 1900s. He and students would spend 3 or 4 months annually studying southern forestry conditions. An early host was the Thompson Lumber Company near Trinity, TX. Henry Hardtner of Urania Lumber Company invited Chapman and the Yale program to work at Urania and developed a camp that facilitated a long-term connection between Urania and Yale. Beginning in 1917 and continuing for several

Professor H.H. Chapman of Yale University led forestry students to Urania for student training for many years.

decades, Chapman led students to install studies in northern Louisiana and southern Arkansas that evaluated reforestation, thinning, effects of fire, and ecology of southern pines.

He pioneered such novel concepts as determining growth possibilities, evaluating the relation of fire to establishment of longleaf pine, and recommending periodic controlled burns as a means of suppressing hardwood competition. Chapman published more than 20 papers between 1909 and the early 1940s dealing with southern pines and their relationship to fire. His work showed that most winter fires do not kill all longleaf pine seedlings; rather, they helped establish stands, suppress pine and hardwood competitors, reduce hazardous fuel accumulation, and control brown-spot disease. Chapman recommended use of fire in longleaf pine stands every 3 years. He has been termed the "father of controlled burning for silvicultural purposes."

The 1917 class of Yale University's School of Forestry at Urania Lumber Company's summer camp site. H.H. Chapman and Henry Hardtner (from left) are seated in the second row.

Chapman's recommendation of the use of controlled burning in longleaf pine reforestation ran counter to the prevailing understanding at the time. This led to a lengthy conflict between Chapman and Forest Service specialists. In the 1920s, the Forest Service published a technical bulletin that stressed the evils of fire in any form or for any purpose. Chapman responded with articles that described the importance of burning in the management of longleaf pine. Eventually, the Forest Service agreed that Chapman's recommendations for longleaf pine management were appropriate.

Although his work with controlled fire was particularly noteworthy, other studies were also very good. One was the description of a natural hybrid of longleaf and loblolly pine. Locals had long recognized this distinctive tree that assumed the worst characteristics of each parent and called it "bastard" pine. Chappy did critical evaluation of the nature of this cross and in 1922 published a careful botanical description. Since he described the hybrid, he was allowed to name the species. He named the hybrid Sonderegger pine (*X Pinus sondereggerii* Chapm.) after the Louisiana State forester at the time. V.L. Sonderegger was a graduate of the Biltmore Forestry School and served as State forester on two separate appointments. He and Chapman disagreed on a number of issues and folklore has it that the naming was not one of honor, but recognition of the local descriptive name of the cross.

In the 1930s, Chapman initiated studies on the effects of thinning on loblolly pine stand development. His studies showed that yield for normal thinning increased stand yields by about 20 percent due to faster rates of diameter growth. These studies emphasized the advantages of applying thinning techniques to stands of timber. His work also led to numerous studies that refined thinning guidelines and improved yields from plantation establishment.

Chapman's leadership in studying southern pine forestry not only contributed greatly to the development of modern forestry practices, but also resulted in training of numerous foresters, many of whom returned to the South in leadership positions. His efforts made a significant impact on the restoration of forests across the South.

References

Chapman, H.H. 1922. A new hybrid pine (*Pinus palustris x Pinus taeda*). Journal of Forestry. 20: 22-24.

Chapman, H.H. 1926. Factors determining natural reproduction of longleaf pine on cutover lands in LaSalle Parish, Louisiana. Bull. 16. New Haven, CT: Yale University School of Forestry. 44 p.

Louisiana State University School of Forestry

Henry Hardtner of Urania Lumber Company and William Sullivan of Great Southern led the development of forestry in Louisiana and the South in the early 1900s. However, there were only a few foresters in the South in the 1920s and 1930s to expand and apply this developing technology. With exception of the Biltmore Forest School in North Carolina, which functioned as a private academy to provide training in practical forestry, collegiate forestry programs were established in only a few northern universities and in the South at the University of Georgia.

The need for forestry training in Louisiana was recognized as early as 1911 when the first forestry course was taught at Louisiana State University in cooperation with the Louisiana Conservation Commission, Division of Forestry. In 1923, a 2-year forestry curriculum was offered, but it was not until 1925 that a 4-year program was established. Major J.G. Lee, Sr. headed the program and Ralph W. Hayes was one of those added to the faculty in 1926. The Louisiana State University program was the second forestry school in the South—the first was a program at the University of Georgia in 1906.

In 1946, a second school of forestry was established at what is now Louisiana Tech University. It was designed to provide students well suited for employment in forest industry.

MAJOR J.G. LEE, SR.

Major J.G. Lee, Sr., was born in Farmerville, LA, on December 17, 1863. He received a B.S. degree from Louisiana State University (LSU) in 1988, and served as assistant director of the North Louisiana Agricultural Experiment Station during the next 8 years.

Lee, whose nephew was the late Dean Lee of the LSU College of Agriculture, next served as state commissioner of Agriculture and Immigration from 1898 to 1906.

Lee was the first professor of forestry at LSU, appointed in 1910. As early as 1921, he began taking his students into Louisiana forests for first-hand study of forestry in the summer months. The first summer camp was held in 1925 on lands of Great Southern near Bogalusa, LA. In 1927, Great Southern donated 1,012 acres to Louisiana State University for use in connection with the School of Forestry. This area is now known as the Lee Memorial Forest and is the School of Renewable Natural Resources' research forest.

Lee was a major on the staffs of two governors, Samuel D. McEnery and Francis T. Nicholls. He served twice as

Major J.G. Lee was the leader who established a forestry education program in Louisiana. (Photo from LSU School of Renewable Natural Resources)

Louisiana Commissioner in charge of State exhibits at the Buffalo Exposition and for the West Indies Exposition at Charleston, SC, from 1891 to 1892.

He was a trustee of Southwestern Louisiana Institute from 1899 to 1904, and was secretary of the Louisiana Commission for the St. Louis World Exposition in 1903-04. For many years, he served on the forestry advisory boards for a number of State organizations, and was a member of the Southern Forestry Congress.

Because Lee taught the vision of reforestation and its importance to future generations, he was termed a pioneer in reforestation and in advanced methods of horticulture. Under his leadership the LSU forestry curriculum was extended to include a fourth year of study in 1925.

Ralph W. Hayes

Ralph Wesley Hayes completed his forestry training at Iowa State University in 1914. He spent the next 10 years in private forestry and the Indian Service as supervisor of the Chippewa Reservation in Wisconsin and the warm Springs Reservation in Oregon. He also opened the first timber sale for the Apache Indians in McNary, AZ. In 1924, he returned to Iowa State to obtain a master's degree in forestry. He worked for the Forest Service before accepting a position at LSU in 1926. In 1929, Hayes moved to North Carolina State University to teach in their forestry program. He returned to LSU in 1934 to become director of the Forestry School in 1935.

Hayes recruited staff members, expanded the curriculum, and convinced LSU authorities of a need for better facilities. His program measured up to the standards set by the Society of American Foresters, and in 1937 LSU became the first accredited forestry school in the South.

Hayes was known by his students as "Prof" Hayes. During his 32 years at LSU a total of 678 foresters went forth with bachelor's and master's degrees. They were well grounded in the fundamentals of scientific forestry. Oriented in the practical aspects of land management, they were ready to undertake their responsibilities of forestry and land managers in the southern region.

Hayes was a quiet, sincere person who was not easily perturbed. One day one of his forest economics students from 20 years earlier visited the school. He complained to Hayes that he had received a D grade in the course and felt that he should have received a C. Hayes calmly sat down beside him, found his old grade book which showed each of this student's grades. Hayes calculated the grade again and quietly told the fellow, "Yes, I calculated your grade correctly. Your grade still computes to be a D."

The LSU program trained foresters who served in most of the major forestry organizations in Louisiana, and they spread across the South and Nation. The training provided by Hayes and his faculty was highly respected across the country.

As "dean of forestry in Louisiana," Hayes presented a gruff exterior, but was a devout Christian and deeply sincere man. His interests and abilities were engrossed in the training and success of his students—all else was secondary. When Ralph Hayes died at the age of 75, he had built a monument—a monument of men. He did not leave a large financial estate, but left a monument in the lives of 678 former students.

Ralph Hayes led the development of the LSU forestry program for an extended time. (Photo from LSU School of Renewable Natural Resources)

A. BIGLER CROW

A. Bigler Crow was born in Warren, PA, in 1910, but grew up in Pittsburgh, PA where he developed his love for baseball. He often saw major league baseball games and became a life-long fan of the Pittsburgh Pirates.

Crow began his forestry education at the former Pennsylvania State School at Mont Alto. He attended the University of Montana for a year and then transferred to North Carolina State University, where he received the B.S.F. degree with high honors in 1934. He worked for the Forest Service in Missouri and Pennsylvania before entering Yale University in 1940, where he received a master's degree in forestry.

Professor A.B. Crow was highly respected by LSU forestry students. (Photo from LSU School of Renewable Natural Resources)

After working for the Soil Conservation Service and the American Forestry Association's Forest Resource Appraisal Team, Crow was recruited in 1946 by Ralph Hayes, of Louisiana State University, to teach silviculture and forest fire protection. He taught these courses for the next 30 years—until he retired. He also taught two graduate-level courses, Advanced Silviculture of the Southern Pines and Research Methods in Forestry. Crow's excellence in teaching was appreciated by his students and he was awarded one of the first outstanding teacher awards of the LSU College of Agriculture.

During sabbatical leaves or summer breaks, Crow frequently visited forestry organizations throughout the region to stay up-to-date on silvicultural practices in the Southern States. Professor Crow was known for his scholarship, his writing ability, his careful research data collection, his contagious,

enthusiastic lectures, and his ability to communicate clearly with students.

His students long remember his "cut-and-leave" tests, which he gave students in the field. These were used to teach the correct method of thinning southern pine stands. His former students remember him fondly and with gratitude.

Crow was honored by his peers in the forestry profession when in 1975 he was presented the Distinguished Service Award by the Gulf States Section, Society of American Foresters. He was also elected Fellow in the Society of American Foresters and recognized by numerous professional and educational organizations. He retired from LSU in 1976 having taught 744 young men who were graduated as professional foresters.

He addressed the LSU Xi Sigma Pi honorary forestry society and gave these thoughtful comments: "We foresters are deeply committed to the principle of stewardship, which simply means to treat the land, including its soil, water, air, plants and animals, in such a fashion as to leave things as good or better than we found them."

Crow died in 1987 in Baton Rouge, LA and a forestry scholarship was established in his name to support incoming LSU students.

References

Anon. 1966. In memoriam. Forests & People. 16(4): 20.

Blackwell, L.P; Burns, P.Y. 1963. The beginning of forestry education in Louisiana. Forests & People. 13(1): 70-71, 106-107, 114.

Burns, P.Y. 2003. Brief history of education in the LSU School of Renewable Natural Resources 1911-2003. http://rnr.lsu edu/alumni/brief. [Date accessed: November 28, 2008].

Dixon, M. 1953. Pioneer forest school serves the South. Forests & People. 3(1): 32-36.

Shuman, E. 1963. Major J.G. Lee—the educator. Forests & People. 13(1): 22.

Louisiana Tech University
LLOYD P. (BLACK) BLACKWELL

Lloyd P. (Black) Blackwell, a Virginia native, graduated from Lynchburg College in 1931 with a degree in history. After working with the Forest Service in several eastern States, he entered Yale University to obtain a master's degree in forestry. While at Yale he was greatly influenced by Professor H.H. Chapman who pioneered research with southern pines at Urania, LA. After his graduation in 1937, Blackwell moved to Urania to become chief forester for Urania Lumber Company. He remained in this position until he entered in the Navy and served during World War II.

Blackwell soon made an impact on forestry in the State. A significant first was his organization in 1941 of the North

Lloyd (Black) Blackwell, head of Louisiana Tech forestry.

Louisiana Group, Society of American Foresters. This was the first organized group below the regional sections of the organization. He served as its chair during most of his career. In addition to leading this proactive group to deal with issues of interest and importance to foresters, Blackwell guided it to initiate a study on Louisiana Forest Taxation. This effort led directly to the formation of the Louisiana Forestry Association in 1946. It was no surprise that Blackwell served as the first executive director until a permanent office could be established. Also, he helped write the bylaws and organize the association.

Another first for Blackwell was serving as chair of the Louisiana Tree Farm Committee, and in that capacity he helped formulate a program that has been cited as a model throughout the Nation.

It was in 1946 that Blackwell went to Louisiana Polytechnic Institute (now Louisiana Tech University) at Ruston to organize and head a department of forestry, the position he held for 30 years. Under Blackwell's direction, in 1955 LA Tech became the second accredited forestry school in the Nation offering only undergraduate work, and the first program of its kind in the South.

Endearingly called "Black" by his friends, he shaped and inspired many. He took a genuine interest in his students, and the LA Tech forestry program was noted for developing and producing students ideally suited for working in forest industry. Blackwell's successful formula included three simple points: teach them to live with people, make good citizens, and make foresters of them.

As an instructor and speaker Blackwell never tried to soften his delivery. Those who knew him acknowledged that he was opinionated and spoke frankly. He was "a fiery soul and a champion for things that he believed in." His flair for the dramatic came from 8 years of speech and drama training in high school and college. Aiding him in his speech were his arms which he used to gesture avidly. Most grew accustomed to his preaching issues he believed in like an old-time circuit rider.

Blackwell's contributions to the development of forestry and the people practicing forestry are innumerable. Edward Kerr, speaking about Blackwell, concluded, "Some people dislike him, some don't know whether they do nor not. One thing is sure though: Everyone knows him!" None would disagree that forestry is a better profession because of the good this man has accomplished.

References

Anon. 1968. The faces of forestry: Lloyd Blackwell. Forests & People. 18(2): 24.

Anon. 1987. A tribute to Black. Forests & People. 37(3): 10-11.

Kerr, E.; Morgan, E. 1955. Prince of Yale's. Forests & People. 5(2): 22-26, 54-55.

University of Arkansas at Monticello
HENRY H. (HANK) CHAMBERLIN

Henry (Hank) Chamberlin was born in 1913 and received a degree in forestry from Pennsylvania State University. He was granted a master's degree in forestry from Yale University in 1940 and became a faculty member at Louisiana State University's School of Forestry in 1941. In the 1943 issue of the School's *Annual Ring*, he is mentioned in the report of the 1942 Summer Camp: "Then came Dendrology with Prof. Chamberlin. He really put us

Hank Chamberlin at his retirement ceremony. (Photo from University of Arkansas, Monticello, School of Forestry Web site)

through the mill in this course, with some 80 different species, leaf mounts and scientific names…The arguments of Prof. Chamberlin versus the class on species of oak was also very much a part of the course."

In 1944, Chamberlin was approached about starting a forestry program in Arkansas. In 1945, Chamberlin decided to leave his position at Louisiana State University to start a 2-year forestry program at Arkansas A&M University in Monticello, AR but he said that he would stay only one year. When he arrived eager to build a 2-year forestry program, he found virtually no resources for supporting the program. So, he worked with what he had. This meant drawing upon his personal qualities to make the unlikely happen.

During his first year, Chamberlin recruited two faculty members. He spent long hours in the classroom, ran the 10-week summer camp, and served as a combination administrator, instructor, fund raiser, and transportation director, shuttling students to and from the field in an old truck. His students remember the truck, which had a stake-sided bed with benches on both sides. Chamberlin maintained he had an excellent record as a truck driver, no accidents, but tires blew out and a wheel fell off.

Chamberlin was a hard worker, pursued excellence, had a sense of urgency, was tenacious, and blended these qualities with a sense of humor. Perhaps most of all, he liked his students, wanted to teach students, and wanted his students to succeed.

With encouragement of students and support of industry, the program expanded from the 2-year curriculum to a 4-year program in 1950. The program continued to grow and space remained a problem. In 1957, the program moved into a new forestry building. Arkansas A&M became the University of Monticello (UAM) when it joined the University of Arkansas System in 1971. The forestry program was first accredited by the Society of American Foresters in 1984, thanks to Chamberlin's groundwork.

Even after Chamberlin stepped down as head of the UAM's School of Forest Resources in 1972, he continued to teach until 1980. From 1945 to 1980, Chamberlin taught all 586 students who graduated from the Arkansas forestry program. He had a tremendous impact on forestry education in Arkansas. Many of those students worked in southern Arkansas, Oklahoma, Mississippi, Louisiana, and Texas, seeing that cutover virgin forest areas were reforested. Chamberlin set a good example for these men.

The man who said he would stay but one year stayed a bit longer. Chamberlin arrived as a "pioneer" and retired as a "classic" 35 years and 5 presidents later. At his retirement, Bob Blackmon, his successor, stated, "Frequently students do not realize until years later that a particular professor has made a significant contribution to his or her educational experience. Not so with Hank Chamberlin. His students recognize his special qualities from their first contact and soon learn to respect him as a teacher and as a human being."

References

Anon. 2009. History of the School. School of Forest Resources, University of Arkansas at Monticello. http://www.afrc.uamont edu/sfr/history.htm. [Date accessed: June 19, 2009].

FOREST PRODUCTS

To lumbermen, second-growth pine stands seemed to offer little promise as a forest resource. The fast growth of these young stands produced lumber of significantly different quality than the old-growth stands. They saw products from such trees as offering little potential in the marketplace. However, a cadre of individuals began a campaign to demonstrate that there was value in this young material.

One of the leaders of this effort was Charles Herty. Before Herty began his crusade to show that newsprint could be an important forest product, he had already improved techniques to collect resin in naval stores operations. Also, he had gained national recognition as a chemist. As Herty was working to convince investors of the potential in paper making, Ralph Lindgren worked on solving the problem of blue stain on lumber.

About three decades later, Peter Koch began to show important progress in developing new products from forest resources. Profiles of these remarkable scientists follow.

Mr. Pulp and Paper of the South

Charles H. Herty

Charles H. Herty, an internationally recognized chemist, revolutionized the southern forestry and naval stores industry. He was born in Milledgeville, GA, in 1867. He earned a bachelor of philosophy degree from the University of Georgia in 1886, and a doctorate from John Hopkins University in 1890.

After working in many positions, various universities, associations and industries, Herty began an effort to develop natural resources of the South. His first approach was to study the naval stores industry's use of longleaf and slash pine to produce timber and turpentine. As a staff member of the U.S. Bureau of Forestry, he perfected the cup and gutter system that became the standard used in the naval stores industry. Prior to use of cups and gutters, resin was collected from living pines trees in a deep hole called a "box"

Charles Herty's efforts related to development of a paper industry in the South are extraordinary. (Photo from Wikipedia Web site)

chopped into the base of each tree worked. Herty's method replaced the chopped box with a clay cup attached to the tree by a single nail. This enabled trees as small as 7 to 8 inches in diameter to be worked as compared with a minimum of 18 to 20 inches with the old box method. By making millions of additional trees available to gum producers, the Herty system revitalized a sagging industry and naval stores became the primary product from the pine forests over much of the Southern Coastal Plain.

After a number of years as president of the American Chemical Society and in other highly influential positions that led to the establishment of the National Institute of Health, Herty returned to the South. He envisioned that a white paper and newsprint industry could be developed using southern pines that could compete with Canadian and northern species. The belief was that the high resin content of pines made the wood unusable for pulping. Herty was convinced that the thousands of acres of new plantations presented a resource to grow a major new industry in the South. He began working to secure funding for an experimental pulp and paper laboratory where he could test his theories regarding substituting cheap, fast-growing southern pine for expensive, slow-growing northern spruce.

At this time there were a few pulp and paper mills in the South (the mill at Bogalusa, LA was one of the first) that used groundwood (mechanical pulp) technology. These mills could not compete in producing high quality paper products because of the high resin content of pine species.

In 1931, he managed to secure an appropriation from the Georgia legislature and a matching grant from the Chemical Foundation, for a facility with free power from the City of Savannah to house the "Savannah Pulp and Paper Laboratory." There Herty and his staff spent several years answering the technical questions that had to be addressed before any manufacturer would invest the millions of dollars necessary to build the South's first newsprint mill.

Herty's work outside the Savannah laboratory was demanding. He spent most of his time traveling, addressing technical societies, pulp and paper manufacturers, and bankers and chambers of commerce to advise them of the success of the laboratory. He urged them to invest in a new industry that, he predicted, would be only the first step in building a "New South."

Herty was a superb showman with a genius for publicity. After he developed confidence in his ability to make newsprint from southern pines, he went all over the South crusading against wood fires. He pointed out that thousands of jobs would be available if a new pine crop was grown for the newly developing newsprint industry. His work provided the pulp and paper industry with a vast source of fiber, and significantly increased the manufacturing base of the Southern States.

The Kraft sulphate pulping process was not one of Herty's developments. The one responsibility for this development was Ed Mayo who also worked in Savannah, GA. However, Herty's efforts contributed significantly to the expansion of the Kraft paper mills.

Tired and exhausted from constant traveling, speech making, appearances before State legislatures, as well as running his laboratory, Herty died in 1938. He received medals from a number of national organizations, plus honorary doctorates from Colgate University, Oglethorpe University, University of Pittsburgh, University of Georgia, University of North Carolina, University of Florida, and Duke University. In 1940, the Charles H. Herty Memorial Highway was dedicated and in 1943, the Liberty Ship S.S. Charles H. Herty was launched. The Herty Medal established by the American Chemical Society is the South's most distinguished award for its chemists. Herty revolutionized the southern forestry and naval stores industries. Few men have contributed more to the development of the South's forest industries than he.

References

Heyward, F. 1963. Charles Herty—Mr. Pulp and Paper. Forests & People. 13(1): 28-29.

Maunder, E.R. 1977. Voices from the South: recollections of four foresters; Inman F. Eldredge, Elwood L. Demmon, Walter H. Damtoft, Clinton H. Coulter. Santa Cruz, CA: Forest History Society, Inc. 252 p.

Read, G.M. 1995. Realization of a dream: Charles H. Herty and the South's first newsprint mill. Forest & Conservation History. 39: 4-16.

Control of Blue-Stain Fungus

Ralph M. (Lindy) Lindgren

Ralph M. (Lindy) Lindgren was detailed to the Southern Station in New Orleans, LA on August 1, 1928, by the old Bureau of Plant Industry after completing his master's degree in plant pathology at the University of Minnesota. He was selected for the position because of his ability and the subject of his thesis. Lindy was assigned the task of coming up with techniques to control blue-stain fungus in freshly sawed lumber. Blue stain was a major economic problem for lumbermen. Under the conditions of high humidity and temperature that is common in the South, the sap wood of pine lumber would be severely stained if not promptly kiln dried. This staining would significantly degrade lumber quality and value.

Lindgren evaluated about 250 potential chemicals on billets of sap pine. He placed treated and untreated samples in the best "blue-stain environment" he could find, namely underneath stacks of green lumber in the yards of a number of saw mills. He found several chemicals that showed promise and used these results to convince companies in Florida, Alabama, Mississippi, and Louisiana to try his six most promising chemicals on carload lots of green lumber.

After a long drought period where no stain developed, a rainy period produced a heavy amount of blue stain. One of Lindgren's chemicals resulted in complete control of the stain. The chemical, ethyl mercury chloride, marketed under the trade name of Lignasan quickly was accepted as a preventive treatment in sawmills. Unheated vats were installed in the green-chain of mills to dip lumber in the chemical solution. One year after the initial report of its effectiveness, the chemical was in use in more than 100 mills.

Ralph Lindgren's work with blue stain gained the Southern Forest Experiment Station much recognition.

Four years from the start, it was in worldwide use. Chapman Chemical Company grew out of the findings.

This one research accomplishment, more than any other single achievement, gained the Southern Station considerable recognition and support.

Lindgren was director of the Station's Division of Plant Pathology when he was transferred in 1952 to head the Forest Products Laboratory in Madison, WI. He resigned from the laboratory in 1962, as chief of the Division of Wood Preservation.

Lindgren's imagination, research ability, personality, and drive led to this significant accomplishment early in his career.

References

Lindgren, R.M ; Verrall, A.F. 1950. Fungus control in unseasoned forest products. Forest Farmer. 9(5): 53-54.

Wakeley, P.C. 1964. A biased history of the Southern Forest Experiment Station through fiscal year 1933. Unpublished document. New Orleans, LA: On file with: USDA Forest Service, Southern Research Station, Forest Management Research, Pineville, LA 71360.

Wakeley, P.C. 1978. The adolescence of forestry research in the South. Journal of Forest History. 22 (7): 135-145.

Timber Harvesting

Albert E. (Wack) Wackerman

Albert (Wack) Wackerman of Cleveland, OH, earned an undergraduate degree from the University of Minnesota in 1921 and a master's degree from Yale University School of Forestry in 1922. He began his professional career in 1923 as a junior forester and assistant silviculturist with the Forest Service, Lake States Experiment Station. In 1927, he joined the Crossett Lumber Company in Arkansas.

One of the first major jobs for the company was to set up a fire protection system and carry out a cruise of two areas of older cutover lands. He was to determine the amount of second-growth pine and hardwood present, its growth and mortality, and the amount of virgin timber remaining. He would then prepare possible management and cutting plans.

Wackerman determined that growth of advance second-growth stands would be such that in 10 years hence the merchantable volume would have grown back to the original amount and another cut could be made. He began the process of preparing management and cutting plans for the company. However, in 1929, the effects of the great depression were being felt by southern pine lumber industry. Reduction in his salary of 50 percent was made, but a year later, in desperation, the company reduced his salary by another 50 percent.

Albert Wackerman was recognized internationally for his work on timber harvesting systems.

Wackerman was more than willing to accept on offer of employment by the Southern Station, so during 1933 and 1934 he was with the Station in Crossett, AR. While there, he played a major part in arranging cooperation between the Crossett Company and the Forest Service, including the donation of the Crossett Experimental Forest to the Southern Station. He also established the original Crossett experiment in all-aged management and launched Reynolds on his career.

After leaving the Forest Service, he had short assignments with the Southern Pine Association in New Orleans and the Seaboard Railroad. In 1938, Wackerman was appointed professor of forest utilization at Duke University. During World War II, he was an advisor to the Office of Price Administration. He served the rest of his career at Duke.

His most important single accomplishment was the publication of "Harvesting Timber Crops" in 1949. This textbook was used in forestry schools across the United States and even in a number of other countries. A second edition with coauthors W.D. Hagenstein and A.S. Michell was published in 1966 and quickly went out of print. No other text replaced the information provided by Wackerman's book, so it was reprinted in India by a book company in 2002 and continues to be distributed worldwide.

He was active professionally, serving as chair of the Gulf States Section of the Society of American Foresters (SAF) in 1934. In 1950, he was chair of the Appalachian Section of the SAF. Wackerman was elected fellow of the SAF in 1961. Shortly before his death, he was accorded special recognition by the Gulf States Section of SAF for his contributions to the forestry profession.

References

Anon. 1980. Obituaries: Albert E. Wackerman. Journal of Forestry. 78: 592.

Reynolds, R.R. 1980. The Crossett story: the beginning of forestry in southern Arkansas and northern Louisiana. Gen. Tech. Rep. SO-32. New Orleans: U.S. Department of Agriculture, Forest Service, Southern Forest Experiment Station. 40 p.

Wackerman, A E. 1949. Harvesting timber crops. New York: McGraw-Hill Book Company. 437 p.

Wakeley, P.C. 1964. A biased history of the Southern Forest Experiment Station through fiscal year 1933. Unpublished document. New Orleans, LA: On file with: USDA Forest Service, Southern Research Station, Forest Management Research, Pineville, LA 71360.

Premier Wood Scientist

PETER KOCH

Peter Koch was one of America's most eminent scientists in wood technology and led the development of equipment and technology that has become the backbone of modern forest industry in the South.

After completing his Ph.D. at the University of Washington in 1954, then 2 years of teaching and research at Michigan State University, and 5 years of managing a New England lumber company, he wrote the book "Wood Machining Processes" based on his development of high-speed chipping technology.

In 1963, Koch was hired to head the new forest products utilization laboratory at the Forest Service, Southern Station's facility at Pineville, LA. Here, in 1963, he cooperated with two machine manufacturers to develop three

Peter Koch's research program changed the forest products industry in the South and influenced national efforts.

versions of chipping headrigs which made logs square by converting the round sides into pulp chips, creating no slabs and wasting no material as sawdust. They are now in wide industrial use throughout North America and comprise one of the major wood-machining advances of the 20th century.

During 1964, as manufacture of southern pine plywood was being developed, Koch provided data instrumental to the formation of gluing practices for the new industry. Next, he developed a system of gluing up single-species wooden beams with the most limber laminate in the central and the stiffest in the outer, most highly stressed regions. Beams thus assembled are stronger, stiffer, and more uniform than those arranged conventionally. For these three developments he was awarded in 1968 the Superior Service medal of the U.S. Department of Agriculture. In less than 5 years, Koch's research resulted in technology that made southern forest products industry competitive on the world market.

During this period, Koch invented a widely applied method of drying southern pine 2 x 4 studs in 24 hours while restraining them so they are straight when dry. He also led a team effort, in which his personal research played an important part, in developing a structural flakeboard from mixed southern hardwoods—including 60 percent by weight of dense oaks and hickories; start-up of the first commercial plant using the process occurred in 1983. This technology became the basis of the Oriented Strand Boards plants that use low-quality hardwood material that was largely underutilized.

Koch's widely used two-volume reference text "Utilization of the Southern Pines" was published as Agricultural Handbook 420 in 1972. These books were a major effort by Peter and the staff of his Research Work Unit. Peter typically worked long hours—up to 18 per day—and assigned chapters for his scientists to produce. It was a significant accomplishment that remains today as a source for detailed information about southern pine wood resources and products.

In 1973, he developed the concept of severing the lateral roots of trees, and then pulling them with a central root mass intact for use in the production of energy, pulp and paper, or naval stores; numerous machines employing the concept were put into commercial operation. In 1974, he conceived a machine that would clean up logging slash comprised of tops and branches, standing culls, and stumps. Through his team leadership the concept was brought to commercial prototype stage in 1978.

Also in 1978, a commercial-scale prototype suspension burner for wet wood and bark, which Koch co-invented, was successfully tested. By 1980, the Abstract Information Digest Service of the Forest Products Research Society, which he initiated, matured as an economically viable computerized information retrieval system for the forest products industry.

Koch served as president of the Forest Products Research Society; and was elected Fellow in the International Academy of Wood Science, and Fellow in the Society of American Foresters. Other recognitions of the esteem in which he was held by his profession include an honorary doctor of science degree from the University of Maine, a John Scott Award, a Woodworking Digest Award, and a Society of American Foresters' Lifetime Achievement Award.

Upon completion of the three-volume work "Utilization of Hardwoods Growing on Southern Pine Sites" in 1982, Koch concluded his Forest Service work in the South. This work on hardwoods was done with the same thoroughness as the earlier work with pine. Koch transferred to the Rocky Mountain Research Station in Missoula, MT, to work on the wood properties and utilization of lodgepole pine. His three-volume "Lodgepole Pine in North America" (1995) text provides an accumulation of resource and product information for this species.

Koch died in 1998. He left a remarkable list of credits and accomplishments. But probably his most gratifying is his legacy to the forest industry in the South. Our modern forest industry is to a large extent built on accomplishments resulting from his ingenuity and hard work.

References

Duffy, I.T. 1975. Faces of forestry—Peter Koch. Forests & People. 25(1): 26-29.

Main, P. 1981. Useful products from an unused resource. Forests & People. 31(2): 12-16.

FOREST RESOURCES

Early foresters in the South were faced with massive reforestation problems, lack of products for second-growth forests, and many other issues that required initiative and dedication of scarce resources. For example, soil erosion was a major problem in hill country where farming had been abandoned. Wildfire was a serious concern and control was believed to be avoided. Range management was needed to limit the losses of new plantations to cattle and hogs. These and other issues required study and development of technology to restore forest land productivity.

Fortunately, a number of individuals led the effort to resolve these major problems and made remarkable progress limiting the negative influence of these on restoration of southern forest ecosystems.

Soil Erosion and Flood Control

H.G. (Mac) Meginnis

Harvest of the pine overstory and failure of agriculture on the rolling hills of north Mississippi and Tennessee resulted in massive erosion and flood problems. A 1930 survey of several counties in north Mississippi showed nearly 35 percent in active gullies, from a foot or two to 80 or 100 feet deep. Similar problems occurred in the hill country across the South, but usually to a smaller degree.

In 1929, H.G. (Mac) Meginnis was recruited by the Southern Station to work on the problems of soil erosion and flood control. Due to the scope of the problem in north Mississippi, Meginnis established headquarters at Holly Springs, MS, and made arrangements for experimental use of an old, badly gullied field. He worked largely single-handed with visits of guidance, advice, and assistance. He depended on temporary local labor for help.

His research, which was both basic and applied, was exemplary. He devised small plots, surrounded by wide strips of galvanized iron with the lower edges sunk into the ground, where he obtained data on erosion and run-off on several soil types, on several degrees of slope, on bare surfaces, and under both grass and tree cover. Meginnis early established that soil protected by leaf litter had very little erosion and run-off compared to bare soil. These results established his reputation and demand for his research information.

The magnitude of erosion and flooding problems and success of Meginnis' work resulted in job offers from other agencies and universities. Since he was the Forest Service's sole specialist in the South, he was promoted from junior forester P-1 to full silviculturist P-4 to keep him.

Meginnis, with approval, purchased a small abandoned chicken house for about $5 to place on his site to use as a laboratory. It was heavily infested with chicken lice. To rid the lice, he purchased some insecticidal spray for 75 cents. This expenditure was disallowed on his expense account by the General Accounting Office on grounds that getting rid of the distracting lice was for the personal benefit of the employee, not for the benefit of the government. How times have changed!

At the time of his work, locust trees were recommended for erosion control plantings. Meginnis' results showed that planting pine

Mac Meginnis standing in a gully formed by soil erosion.

seedlings was more effective and they would survive, grow on a wider array of sites, and provide valuable products. His data resulted in establishment of a congressionally funded program, the Yazoo-Little Tallahatchie (Y-LT) Flood Prevention Project. This program, started in 1948, continued for more than 25 years to rehabilitate 835,900 acres of highly eroded lands in north Mississippi. It has been called the Forest Service's largest tree-planting project.

"Mac" Meginnis developed techniques to stabilize the highly eroded soils of north Mississippi and Tennessee. His work was recognized worldwide.

After Meginnis established his guidelines for gully restoration, he was transferred to the Appalachian Forest Experiment Station in Asheville, NC. There he continued his efforts in understanding the effects of forests in controlling erosion and flood damage in mountainous terrain. Meginnis was highly regarded by his contemporaries and almost single-handed developed guidelines for restoring some of the South's most devastated lands.

References

Meginnis, H.G. 1933. Tree planting to reclaim gullied lands in the South. Journal of Forestry. 31: 649-656.

Meginnis, H.G. 1935. Effect of cover on surface run-off and erosion in the loessial uplands of Mississippi. Circulator 347. Washington, DC; U.S. Department of Agriculture. 15 p.

Wakeley, P.C. 1964. A biased history of the Southern Forest Experiment Station through fiscal year 1933. Unpublished document. New Orleans, LA: On file with: USDA Forest Service, Southern Research Station, Forest Management Research, Pineville, LA 71360.

Prescribed Fire

H.H. (CHAPPY) CHAPMAN

The history of fire in southern forests is a long and vexing one. Firing the woods has been a common practice in the South. Some described it as natural as honking of migrating geese or appearance of crimson foliage on sweet gums (Heyward 1958). American Indians had long used fire to maintain open forests to facilitate hunting and even used fire to drive deer through openings where they were more easily harvested.

Settlers used fire to clear land and to "green up" the grass in the spring to provide new growth for their grazing animals. Such practices were particularly common on the cutover forest land that provided open range for their cattle. However, early foresters found need to control fires if reforestation efforts were to be successful. One of the first specific forest practices to be undertaken in the South had to do with fire protection. The first large-scale attempts to control fire were on national forests.

The American Forestry Association awakened much interest in early fire protection in 1929 by sending a caravan of trucks into the South to begin a 3-year crusade for fire protection. Equipped with moving pictures and literature, trucks roved the hinterlands in several States where fire problems were severe. Known as the "Dixie Crusaders", these members of fire prevention caravans traveled 300,000 miles through the Deep South, holding rallies, distributing pamphlets, and showing self-produced movies to some three million people.

This effort was particularly effective because motion pictures were shown in areas where they were not generally available. Many meetings were held outdoors because no building was usually adequate to hold the crowd. One of the lecturers is quoted as saying, "Many of the people who came never before had seen a motion picture—some had never heard of such a thing."

John F. Shea, a psychologist, was hired by the Forest Service to study why locals set fires. He reported at the time that many of the people craved excitement in "an environment otherwise barren of emotional outlets" (Kerr 1958). Maybe this was why Dixie Crusaders were successful, their effort created a lot of interest because it was so unique for its time.

Fire protection became a moral crusade and early Forest Service researchers were generally proponents for complete control of fire. However, based on his research with the Urania Lumber Company, H.H. (Chappy) Chapman became a proponent of controlled use of fire as a means of controlling wildfires and, more importantly, stimulating forest regeneration of southern pines. In a 1912 article, Chapman argued that to keep fire entirely out of southern pine lands might result in complete destruction of the forests. Later, in 1926, he issued his famous Yale University School of Forestry Bulletin 16 which caused controversy among southern foresters because he called for the use of fire in longleaf pine regeneration (Chapman 1926).

Chapman, who brought the Yale University School of Forestry seniors to Urania several months a year for decades, became a champion of controlled burning. He performed research demonstrating that southern pines rely on fire to suppress hardwood competitors, reduce hazardous fuel buildup, and control brown-spot disease of longleaf pine. Chapman stoutly defended his position in letters published in the Journal of Forestry. For a number of years, Forest Service foresters rebutted his position.

Professor H.H. Chapman measuring a longleaf seedling affected by fire.

In 1928, Phil Wakeley and others of the Southern Station began a large study to evaluate Chapman's contentions. With one exception, they found that Chapman's positions were correct. They did conclude that burning did not protect longleaf seedlings from brown-spot needle disease of longleaf pine. Gradually, foresters accepted Chapman's conclusions and became advocates of controlled or prescribed burning.

Chapman was a charismatic but forceful character. He published more than 20 papers between 1909 and the early 1940s dealing with southern pines and their relationship to fire. His work showed that most winter fires do not kill all longleaf pine seedlings; but they helped establish pine stands, suppress pine and other hardwood competitors, and reduce hazardous fuel accumulations. Chapman recommended use of fire in longleaf pine every 3 years. For his pioneering work, he has been termed the "father of controlled burning for silvicultural purposes."

References

Chapman, H.H. 1926. Factors determining natural reproduction of longleaf pine on cutover lands in LaSalle Parish, Louisiana. Bulletin 16. New Haven, Connecticut: Yale University School of Forestry. 44 p.

Clark, T.D. 1984. The greening of the South: the recovery of land and forest. Lexington, KY: The University Press of Kentucky. 168 p.

Kerr, Ed. 1958. History of forestry in Louisiana. Baton Rouge, LA: Louisiana Forestry Commission. 55 p.

Komarek, E.V. 1973. Ancient fires. In: Proceedings Annual Tall Timbers Fire Ecology Conference. Tallahassee, FL: Tall Timbers Research Station: 13: 219-241.

Wildlife Conservation

Issues related to wildlife conservation developed slowly as an offshoot of forestry. Initially, the study of animals in forest settings was called game management. Emphasis on animals centered on those that were commonly harvested for food or for sport. With time a number of significant species dwindled and both hunters and sportsmen began to understand that game management should be broadened to understand the interactions of hunting large animals and forest practices on a whole array of species and their environment.

Wildlife conservation began to focus on species that had little interest to the hunter or sportsman. Even small song birds were found to become indicators of the health of a forest ecosystem. It is noteworthy that our understanding of environmental change was led by those studying the habitat of wildlife species. Individuals who are profiled here led the development of that new understanding.

BRYANT A. BATEMAN

Bryant Bateman was born in 1900 on a farm near Franklinton, LA, and graduated from the public schools there. He attended Louisiana State University for a year, and then taught in Washington Parish schools for 3 years. He returned to LSU in 1923 and graduated in 1926 with a degree in forestry. He was likely influenced by his older brother, F.O. (Red) Bateman, who without much formal education, became ranger for Great Southern and led the development of nursery and reforestation practices for that company (see profile on Bateman). Bryant was employed by Great Southern for a few years after his graduation from LSU in 1926. As a forester, he was involved in tree planting, timber estimating, fire suppression, growth studies, and land surveying. He became a licensed land surveyor.

Bryant was the first student to graduate from LSU in forestry, and after his work experience at Great Southern, he joined the forestry faculty in Baton Rouge, LA in 1931 as its interim head. He entered graduate school in forestry at Iowa State University and received a master's degree in 1934.

Bateman continued his education at the University of Michigan where he earned a doctorate in forestry and game management. He was a student during 1937 and 1938 and was awarded his degree in 1949.

During World War II, he assumed the duties of extension forester and traveled the State, teaching forest practices to rural residents. His research interests were farm forestry, upland forest wildlife management, use of fire in silviculture and wildlife management.

Bryant Bateman was the first graduate in forestry from Louisiana State University.

In 1947, Bateman became the "father" of LSU's game management (later wildlife) degree program. He was instrumental in bringing Leslie Glasgow to the wildlife faculty in 1948. Bateman taught forestry in the early days of the school, then upland wildlife management. Fishing was his hobby, and he introduced fisheries into the school's academic program. Later he helped bring a fisheries specialist to the facility.

Of particular interest was forest management as habitat for upland game, woodlot management for timber and pine straw, use of fire in forest and wildlife management, and feeding habits of wildlife. His interest in use of pine straw as mulch in the strawberry growing area near Hammond preceded such use as an agroforestry practice. Bateman was, also, an early and strong advocate of prescribed burning.

In 1965, Bateman won both the first Louisiana Governor's State Conservation Award and also the Conservationist of the Year Award (Louisiana Outdoor Writers Association). He served as an advisor to State legislators in wildlife legislation and the Louisiana Department of Wildlife and Fisheries on the management of bottomland hardwood forests as wildlife habitat. In 1972, he was named Alumnus of the Year by the LSU Forestry, Wildlife and Forestry Alumni Association. He helped organize the Louisiana Wildlife Federation and served on its board of directors, as well as a number of other professional organizations.

He retired in 1971 and was named Professor Emeritus. He died in 1984, and in 2004 the Bryant A. Bateman Professorship in Natural Resources was established in the school.

Bateman was known, loved, and respected by hundreds of fellow teachers, former students, professional colleagues, agricultural leaders, farm and forest landowners, and just plain people throughout the South. Colleague Prof. A.B. Crow states of Bryant Bateman, "His dedication to wise land use and harmony of all interests in forest and wildlife management was felt by all who came under his kindly spell. He was a quiet man, had an unequaled sense of fairness, and was strong in conviction but gentle in putting forward his views. He was simply, 'a great man.' "

Claude H. (Grits) Gresham

Claude Gresham, born in 1922, was a native of South Carolina. He attended Blue Ridge School for Boys and the universities of North Carolina, Vanderbilt, and Yale. After serving in the U.S. Army Air Corps in World War II, he entered Louisiana State University School of Forestry, obtaining a B.S.F. degree in 1949 and an M.S. degree in 1950, both degrees in game management.

After graduation, Gresham began work with the Louisiana Wildlife and Fisheries Commission where he became chief of the Information Education Division of the Louisiana Game and Fish Commission. Under his editorship, the *Louisiana Conservationist* magazine was recognized as one of the top wildlife magazines in the country. He resigned this position in 1956 to enter a partnership to establish Wood's Lodge on Black Lake near Campti, LA. At the time, Black Lake was one of the finest fishing spots in the South.

Under the byline of 'Grits Gresham,' he began publishing outdoor material in national publications such as *Outdoor Life*, *Field & Stream*, *Sports Illustrated*, *True*, and *Fisherman*. He became known worldwide as a writer, photographer, book author, and television personality.

He served as field host and producer for ABC television's "The American Sportsman" series, host of ESPN's "Shooting Sports America," and, for 26 years, shooting editor for *Sports Afield*. He may be best known for his role in the series of commercials for Miller Lite Beer. Gresham was the fisherman among the athletes who made "Tastes Great, Less Filling" marketing buzzwords for more than a decade.

With his trademark driftwood, floppy hat and white muttonchops, he traveled the world hunting, shooting, and fishing with some of America's most interesting people. He also spent a lifetime championing key outdoor and environmental issues. He was one of the first public voices bringing attention to the loss of wetlands along the Louisiana coastline, an area where he did much of his graduate work while at LSU. His title for an early story on the problem was "Kiss the Land Goodbye."

Gresham received many awards—some are Winchester Outdoorsman of the Year, Alumnus of the Year in the LSU School of Forestry, Wildlife and Fisheries, and induction into the Louisiana Sports Hall of Fame and LSU Hall of

Gresham became an outdoor icon and pioneer. (Photo Alexandria Town Talk)

Distinction. Also, he received an award for excellence in writing and contributions to conservation from the Outdoor Writers Association of America.

Gresham, who was better know by his nickname, 'Grits,' was an American outdoor icon. He was a noted author and television personality. He moved his background and training in wildlife management into a higher level—a remarkable individual who never forgot the basic values from which he came.

References

Anon. 1956. Gresham forms new business. Forests & People. 6(1): 55.

Anon. 1970. Faces of forestry: Bryant A. Bateman. Forests & People. 20(3): 26, 28.

Burns, P. Y. 2008. Human interest notes about Dr. B.A. Bateman. June 16, 2008. Unpublished document. Baton Rouge, LA: On file with: Louisiana State University, School of Renewable Natural Resources. 3810 West Lakeshore Drive, Baton Rouge, LA 70808.

Timothy, P. 2008. Outdoor icon 'Grits' Gresham dies at age 85. Alexandria, LA: Town Talk, February 19, 2008: A1, A3.

Forest Pathology

George H. Hepting

George H. Hepting was born in Brooklyn, NY, in 1907. He attended Cornell University and received a B.S. degree in forestry in 1929 and a Ph.D. in forest pathology in 1933. Even before he completed his doctorate, he joined scientists in the Department of Agriculture studying the heartrot diseases of forest trees. He determined the impact of fire scars, basal wounds, and stump sprouts on infection and spread of decay in Mississippi Delta hardwoods. He was first to describe the remarkable mechanisms by which trees restrict the development of decay and discoloration in stems.

With his doctorate in hand, Hepting was assigned to the Appalachian Forest Experiment Station—later reorganized and renamed the Southeastern Forest Experiment Station. In 1962, he transferred from the Station's office in Asheville, NC, to the Forest Service's Washington (DC) Office. He retired from the Forest Service in 1971, but remained active as a visiting professor at North Carolina State University's Department of Plant Pathology and School of Forest Resources.

Before and during World War II, he studied fungal discoloration in felled timber and lumber of southern pines. Under Hepting's direction, his small group shifted the emphasis of their work to problems of wood in service. The U.S. Navy and U.S. Coast Guard wanted information on the prevention of decay in wooden boats, and they and the U.S. Army planned to build wooden airplanes and gliders. Furthermore, there were costly wood-decay problems in

buildings, truck bodies, and bridge timbers. Through the efforts of Hepting and his research group, the deterioration problems in wood aircraft were corrected early in the war. The importance of this valuable contribution to the war effort has not been fully recognized.

Hepting grew up in the city environment of Brooklyn, NY but early in his life developed a deep love and scientific interest in forestry. He became America's most skilled scientist in the theory and practice of forest pathology.

Hepting studied how long-lived forest trees, unlike most plants, cope with the long-term changes in their biological, physical, and chemical environments. He devoted his career to learning, understanding, and teaching how trees survive disease stresses in forest nurseries, as individual trees, in young sapling stands, in naturally regenerated and planted stands, in old growth forests, and in landscapes and watersheds.

Few investigators in forest sciences were able in a lifetime to make as many major contributions as Hepting did on a diverse range of complex problems. He had the ability to identify primary causes of deterioration and insight to devise practical approaches for management practices. During his career, he became a recognized and influential international authority for forestry in a broad sense.

Hepting's achievements in science were recognized by many honors and awards. In 1969, he became the first forester elected to the National Academy of Sciences. He also received the U.S. Department of Agriculture's Superior Service Award and the Society of American Foresters'

Henry Hepting, America's premier forest pathologist.

Barrington Moore Award for outstanding achievements in forestry research. He was elected Fellow of the Society of American Foresters and of the American Phytopathological Society.

He was one of the most creative scientists America has produced in the field of forest disease research. He was willing to speak frankly and critically when he thought the occasion demanded. Also, he insisted that his associates maintain the same high standards of scientific integrity and quality that he demanded in his own research. Hepting died in Asheville, NC in 1988.

References

Anon. 1954. G.H. Hepting honored by U.S.D.A. Journal of Forestry. 52(9): 553-554.

Cowling, E.B.; Kelman, A.; Powers, H.R., Jr. 1999. George Henry Hepting: pioneer leader in forest pathology. Annual Review of Phytopathology. 37: 19-28.

Hepting, G.H. 1935. Decay following fire in young Mississippi Delta hardwoods. Tech. Bull. 494. Washington, DC: U.S. Department of Agriculture. 32 p.

Tree Improvement and Genetics

A major limitation of seedling production in the early 1950s was the lack of reliable supplies of high-quality seed from desirable sources. Collections tended to be either from felled trees or from standing trees that were easy to climb. Philip Wakeley's research with pine plantation forestry set the stage for efforts in selecting sources that would improve plantation growth and yield. Geographic variation in seed sources began to be understood and local seed sources were believed to be more appropriate than seed from distant sources. But, it was through development of cooperative tree improvement programs that genetics of forest trees were seriously addressed. Philip Wakeley and Bruce Zobel led the initial efforts in what became large-scale, regional programs of tree improvement and genetics of southern pines.

PHILIP C. (PHIL) WAKELEY

Philip Wakeley began his research of southern pine plantation forestry when he arrived at the Southern Station's office in New Orleans, LA in 1924. Fresh from his academic program at Cornell University, he was assigned to Bogalusa, LA, to conduct collaborative research with J.K. (Jake) Johnson and F.O. (Red) Bateman of Great Southern. This assignment was fortunate. Great Southern was one of the largest and most progressive lumber companies in the South. Wakeley's efforts with their staff of Johnson and Bateman resulted in development of the basic nursery technology that was applied across the South. This technology was further refined in the 1930s when Wakeley's efforts were moved to the Forest Service's Stuart Nursery near Pollock, LA,

which was established in 1934 with resources of the Civilian Conservation Corps (CCC).

During this period, Wakeley and his colleagues planted, with help of CCC employees, about 670,000 seedlings in research studies on the Palustris Experimental Forest. His research, which led to the major research contribution to pine plantation forest in the South, was published in 1954 as "Planting the Southern Pines." In this publication, Wakeley documented the technology that was applied to reforest the South. He also reported a study he installed in 1926 that evaluated effects of four different seed sources on stand productivity. At 15 years in plantation age the local source had produced more than twice as much pulpwood per acre as either of the two most distant sources. In addition, conspicuous and economically important differences in resistance to disease appeared among the different sources.

Wakeley's photographic documentation of the 1926 study's results did much to influence foresters on the importance of seed source selection. The developing interest in seed source influence on productivity created a lot of interest in further studying the effects. One of the first formal steps in this direction came in 1951, when a group of foresters met in Atlanta, GA to develop a tree improvement strategy for the South. This meeting led to the formation of the Southern Forest Tree Improvement Committee (SFTIC). One of the first important undertakings of SFTIC was to establish the Southwide Pine Seed Source Study under the direction of Wakeley.

The Southwide Pine Seed Source Study was a gigantic undertaking. Thirty three of the studies 57 plantations were established during the winter of 1952-53. At each plantation site, seedlings of loblolly, shortleaf, slash, and longleaf pines, representing a wide geographic range of seed-

Phil Wakeley (left) discussing reforestation of longleaf pine with an English visitor.

Results of Wakeley's geographic seed source study published in 1944 convinced many of the importance of seed selection and influenced establishment of the much larger Southwide Pine Seed Source Study and development of major tree improvement programs.

collection sites, were planted. It was a massive undertaking, requiring the cooperation of Federal, State, industrial, and university specialists in spreading the costs and dividing the labor. This large cooperative effort is one of the landmarks in the research on artificial regeneration of southern pines. Wakeley's study proved vital not only to efforts to plant "unimproved" seedlings in areas which they were adapted, but also to designing future tree improvement programs for the region.

The significance of this study can be understood by its description by leading forest pathologists in Washington, DC, who called it a "gift from the gods." They recommended that the outplantings be followed to gain understanding of the biology of insect and disease pests that could affect pine plantation performance.

Results of Wakeley's Southwide Pine Seed Source Study provided the data to develop recommendations for seed sources for particular species and locations across the South. His results show that performance of plantations could be greatly improved by careful selections of seed source. Later results demonstrated still more potential for genetic improvement.

Wakley's contributions to the restoration of pine forests across the South are truly remarkable. His work, also, set the stage for other significant programs in reforestation, tree improvement, and genetics.

BRUCE J. ZOBEL

Bruce J. Zobel was born in California in 1920, the son of a fruit and vegetable farmer. He graduated from the University of California, Berkeley, in 1943, and was drafted soon thereafter into the Marine Corps. This service enabled Zobel to return to college under the GI Bill to earn a master's degree and complete doctoral training.

Bruce Zobel, a creative scientist and gifted teacher of forest tree improvement and genetics. (Photo from txforestservice.tamu.edu)

60

In 1951, Zobel was hired by the Texas Forest Service to head a new tree-improvement program. The effort, which became known as the West Gulf Forest Tree Improvement Program, was the first cooperative tree improvement program of its kind. It was supported by the Texas Forest Service, Texas A&M University, Texas Agricultural Experiment Station, and a number of forest industries. The activities of the cooperative concentrated mostly on areas of drought resistance, seed orchard management, superior tree selection, and genetics of wood specific gravity.

When Zobel started his seed orchard, scientists did not know how to graft pines, how far apart to plant them, or how much and what kind of fertilizer to apply. Because there were no flowering grafts initially, much of the early work was done in the woods on original selections. These were scattered over several States. However, many of the techniques tried were successful and are still in use today.

Zobel's achievements attracted the attention of North Carolina State College (later North Carolina State University), and in 1956, Zobel was asked to establish a similar tree improvement program there. This program, too, was a cooperative effort between Federal, State, university and forest industry professionals. In 1962, Zobel was named E.F. Conger Distinguished Professor of Forestry at North Carolina State University. In addition to running the tree improvement program, Zobel taught courses and advised forestry students on forest improvement and genetics.

Zobel's accomplishments both in research and in development of a fully operational program of providing better trees for industrial forestry in the South have been widely recognized. In 1979, Zobel retired from North Carolina State University, but continued to teach part-time until 2004. He consulted for international forestry firms for several years, and in 1984, he founded Zobel Forestry Associates. Here are a few of the awards that he received: In 1965, Governor's Award for Conservation in North Carolina; in 1968, Barrington Moore Award for biological research from the Society of American Foresters, and Fellow of the International Academy of Wood Sciences; in 1969, Fellow of the Society of American Foresters; in 1973, Fellow and the TAPPI Research and Development Award from the Technical Association of the Pulp and Paper Industry; and in 2004, Alexander Quarles Holladay Medal for Excellence, North Carolina State University.

Zobel is described as a creative scientist and gifted teacher of a large cadre of graduate students. Above all, he has been a professional forester who has contributed greatly to improving the economic efficiency of forestry as a means of serving his fellow Americans.

References

Lantz, C.W.; Kraus, J.F. 1987. A guide to southern pine seed sources. Gen. Tech. Rep. SE-43. Asheville, NC: U.S. Department of Agriculture, Forest Service, Southeastern Forest Experiment Station. 34 p.

Wakeley, P.C. 1944. Geographic seed source of loblolly pine seed. Journal of Forestry. 42: 23-33.

Wakeley, P.C. 1954. Planting the southern pines. Agricultural Monograph 18. Washington, DC: U.S. Department of Agriculture, Forest Service. 233 p.

Wells, O.O; Wakeley, P.C. 1966. Geographic variation in survival, growth, and fusiform rust infection of planted loblolly pine. Forest Science Monographs 11. 40 p.

Zobel, B.J. 1953. Seed orchards for superior trees. Forest Farmer. 13: 10-12, 20.

PHOTOGRAPHY/HISTORY

Soon after the end of World War II, tremendous strides were made in forestry throughout the South. Organizations leading the effort to expand forestry practices began to develop public relations staffs to educate the public about these practices. The responsibility of these groups was to capture new developments by photography. Photographs were used to strengthen a variety of public relations activities, but primarily for use in publications. Excellent photographers were either hired or used on a contract basis. Organizations such as the Louisiana Forestry Commission and the Forest Service developed photographic files that now hold unique and irreplaceable information.

Less frequently, historians began to document the development of forestry and capture the contributions of pioneering organizations and leading individuals. The development of forestry in the United States began slowly in the early 20th century, so few historians looked at its development and influence until the 1960s. Even then, little effort went into recording history of forestry organizations. Anna Burns' documentation of the history of the Louisiana Forestry Commission was a ground-breaking event. James Fickle's historical work of forestry in Mississippi and the South is a contemporary effort (Fickle 2001).

Although photographers and historians were not major contributors to the restoration of the South's forests, they were important in documenting the restoration process. It is then appropriate that they be recognized. They did much to preserve the accomplishments of many pioneering individuals.

Forestry Photography

Forestry is not a field where you frequently find professional photographers. Yet, Louisiana had two who made great contributions to helping develop the public understanding of forestry and the nature that it represents. Both worked for a time with the Louisiana Forest Commission and the Louisiana Forestry Association. They also supported efforts by the Forest Service's Southern Station.

Both contributed to the communication of the condition of the State's forest resources and the need to restore its forests to a productive state. They were not, however, limited to exercising their talents in forestry applications. Their talents went well beyond this narrow scope of interest and included capturing on film many of the unique features of the Louisiana landscape.

TOMMY T. KOHARA

Tommy T. Kohara came from a family of photographers. He moved to central Louisiana as a youngster with his family in the 1920s when lumber companies were trying to bring Midwesterners here to grow truck crops on cutover forest land. The farming experiment lasted just 2 years, after which they moved to Alexandria, LA where the father, a photographer in Iowa, soon had his own studio.

Kohara graduated with a degree in forestry from Louisiana State University in 1939. He worked for the Forest Service in Mississippi on a temporary assignment until the

Tommy Kohara, early forestry photographer.

funding ended. But, it was there that he took his first pictures of forests. He returned to work in his father's studio which was very busy with companies building the huge army camps that ringed the city.

He entered the U.S. Army in 1941 and served in Europe for 4 years taking photographs on the front lines in Germany and France. Back in Alexandria, LA in 1945, he took a job with the Louisiana Forestry Commission and for 10 years traveled the State taking pictures and doing public relations for the Forestry Commission.

His direct connection with forestry ended in 1956 when the Alexandria Daily Town Talk asked him to be their chief photographer. But, his ties with forestry did not end. He was often called upon by forestry agencies for skills as a photographer. His work documented the development of direct seeding technology and many other new forestry accomplishments. Often his photographs were used for the covers of *Forests & People*, a magazine of the Louisiana Forestry Association.

There are legends about his prowess. One has it that he drove with a forester miles out in the woods to get a picture on a cloudy day. Kohara took only one exposure, explaining to his amazed companion that he was sure he had the picture. He did!

Kohara set a standard for quality in forest photography that remains today.

ELEMORE MORGAN, SR.

Elemore Morgan, Sr.'s interest in photography developed late in life. A native of Baton Rouge, LA, Morgan grew up in the Depression and worked as a farmer, managed a B.F. Goodrich store, and became an oil distributor. While working for the Goodrich store, he bought a cheap camera to try to sell the Goodrich company on promoting good roads.

When working as an oil distributor, he developed tuberculosis which destroyed his vocal cords. During the time that he could not speak, Morgan wrote notes to people. During his recovery period, he spent 6 months in Kerrville, TX, learning to talk again. His voice became a soft one, whisperish in pitch, which gave what he said a confidential tone.

Morgan became adept at photography while working for a noted Baton Rouge architect, using photographs to show clients the type of construction feasible. It was inevitable that Morgan would be drawn into forestry. It was an outdoorsman's field where men who knew the soil knew that Louisiana must grow from the roots up for lasting prosperity. Morgan became known for his images of Louisiana landscapes, churches, folk culture, and people.

Morgan developed a relationship with leaders in forestry organizations throughout Louisiana. He worked for *Forests & People*, and his photographs did much to establish it as a premier publication. A number of the photographs shot for this publication earned major awards. However, he had a broader interest in the environment and culture of his native State.

Morgan's early work was included in a 1943 book, "Bayous of Louisiana" by Harnett Kane. In 1950, he collaborated with Frances Parkinson Keyes on a book project titled "All This is Louisiana." Morgan had no formal training as a photographer, but his dramatic photographs became known for their style and power.

Elemore Morgan, Sr., at a book signing of "All This is Louisiana."

He frequently took his son, Elemore, Jr., on his photography travels and instilled in him the love for rural Louisiana. Elemore, Jr., became noted for his colorful paintings of the architecture and panoramic vistas of the prairies of southwestern Louisiana. As a professor at University of Louisiana, Lafayette, Morgan, Jr., influenced and mentored hundreds of artists.

"Rural Landmarks and Life in Louisiana, 1937-1965" was a show of Morgan, Sr.'s work organized by the Alexandria Museum of Art. The exhibition was also shown at Mississippi State University's McComas Hall Art Gallery. This exhibit describes Morgan, Sr. as the "dean of Louisiana landscape" and as "first to recognize that the basis of the South was its agrarian culture, and that even then it was beginning to disappear."

Edward Kerr said of Morgan, Sr., "There were no discouraging words in Elemore's vocabulary. He was a 'can do' photographer who could bring snap to what seemed the most ordinary of scenes to untrained eyes. We looked, but he saw. And his excitement was so contagious; he eventually made us all see as well."

References

Derr, H. 1981. Forestry on film: A profile of Tommy Kohara. Forests & People. 31(4): 19-21.

Kerr, E. 1966. The world of Elemore Morgan. Forests & People. 16(3): 12-13.

Morgan, E. Kerr, E. 1962. The Lower Mississippi Valley: A study in photographs and words. Baton Rouge, LA: Claitor's Book Store. [no pagination].

Tompkins, J. 1997. Forestry in black and white. Forests & People. 47(2): 30.

Forestry History

History can be documented in a number of ways. One is for trained historians to take a backward look at those who contributed to the development of our industry, society, and culture. Anna Burns' work which follows the development of forestry in Louisiana is such a traditional approach.

Another approach is one demonstrated by Edward Kerr. He documented in journal articles the significant contributions of many near the end of their careers or in their obituaries. Though not an effort thorough in scope, this approach does record much relevant historical information that would otherwise be lost.

EDWARD F. (ED) KERR, SR.

Edward (Ed) Kerr was born in Baton Rouge, LA , in 1921. He obtained degrees in arts from Louisiana State University and in journalism from the University of Missouri. His early employment was with newspapers in Baton Rouge, LA, but he served as press representative for the Louisiana Forestry Commission from 1951 to 1959. Here he gained a solid

Ed Kerr, writer extraordinary.

background in forestry operations and personalities throughout the State.

Kerr became assistant executive director of the Louisiana Forestry Association in 1959 and assumed the editorial responsibility for *Forests & People*. He served in this capacity only 3 years, but during that time he gained national acclaim for the excellence of this publication.

A hallmark of his tenure as editor of *Forests & People* was the emphasis on history of forestry with a focus on those individuals who led the restoration of the South's forests. Of particular note was the 1963 issue which focused on the 50th anniversary of forestry in Louisiana. Another recurring theme was 'Faces of Forestry,' featuring leaders of forestry. These emphases did much to document those who contributed significantly to the development of forestry in the South.

While associated with the Louisiana Forestry Association, he partnered with Elemore Morgan, an outstanding photographer, to document the nature of forests and those individuals who worked in them. Kerr's words with Morgan's photographs captured the essence of the rural South.

After resigning as assistant executive director in 1962, Kerr continued as editor of *Forests & People* until 1964. At this time, he accepted a public relations position in the information office of the U.S. Department of Interior in Washington, DC. Later he was selected as chief of technical publications for the U.S. Forest Service's State and Private Office in Atlanta, GA. In 1975, Kerr became chief of the information and publications group of the Southern Station in New Orleans, LA.

Kerr was the recipient of numerous regional and national awards. He excelled in all his assignments, but writing was his forte. He was described as "understanding the depth of forestry problems in the South, and having ability to reduce complex thoughts to simple, easy to understand language. His understanding of people was a tremendous value to the organizations for which he worked."

ANNA C. BURNS

Henry Hardtner's dogged determination to apply forestry principles to his land holdings in north Louisiana and to Louisiana in general led to the establishment of forestry organizations early in the 20th century. A State forestry organization was established in principle by Louisiana's legislature in 1904. However, this legislation was far ahead of its time. This and foresighted efforts promoted by Hardtner established a rich legacy for historians.

Anna Maria Cannaday Burns accepted the challenge of documenting this history. Born in Memphis, TN, she entered H. Sophie Newcomb College in New Orleans in 1940. When her family moved to Baton Rouge, LA she transferred to Louisiana State University where she earned a bachelor of arts degree in history and a bachelor of science degree in library science. After teaching in several public school systems, she and her husband, Edmond Burns, moved to Alexandria, LA where she became assistant librarian at Louisiana State University at Alexandria.

Influenced by her husband's employment as a staff forester with the Louisiana Forestry Commission, Burns entered Northwestern State College in Natchitoches to obtain a master of arts degree in history. For her thesis, she began an effort to document the history of the Louisiana Forestry Commission. When conferring with another historian about her topic, she was asked, "Why would you want to do that?" At the time there was little interest in history of such a State forestry organization.

Dr. Anna Burns, librarian at LSU at Alexandria and noted forestry historian.

Burns' thesis was published as "A History of the Louisiana Forestry Commission," and it gained her recognition as a forestry historian. She then began work on a doctorate at the University of Southwestern Louisiana in Lafayette, LA. The topic for her dissertation research was history of the Kisatchie National Forest. The information she documented in these efforts presented opportunities for publishing a number of articles that focused on interesting individuals or organizations. One of the most noted was her documentation of Henry Hardtner's contributions to forestry.

She has served on the Board of Directors of the Forest History Society and now is a director of the Louisiana Maneuvers History Museum at Camp Beauregard in Pineville, LA. Also, she was a member of the International Union of Research Organizations' History Section, and she attended two of the organization's meetings, one in Yugoslavia.

Burns retired as librarian of Louisiana State University at Alexandria a number of years ago, but she still has interest is historic issues related to forestry. Of great interest to her are the contributions of Civilian Conservation Corps (CCC) projects in Louisiana. She has collected information about CCC camps and projects and interviewed numerous individuals who worked in the program. A goal is to document the contributions of this program to the development of forestry in the State. As Burns says, "Efforts of CCC boys had a lasting influence on developing forestry and economic recovery following the Great Depression."

Burns has done much to help the public understand the richness of our forestry heritage. Through her efforts, individuals who have established and developed forestry programs have come alive again and their contributions to society have not been lost.

References

Burns, A.C. 1968. A history of the Louisiana Forestry Commission. Monograph Series, Number One. Natchitoches, LA: Northwestern State College, Louisiana Studies Institute. 137 p.

Burns, A.C. 1978. Henry E. Hardtner: Louisiana's first conservationist. Journal of Forest History. 22(2): 79-85.

Burns, A.C.; Couch, R.W. 1994. A history of the Kisatchie National Forest. Pineville, LA: U.S. Department of Agriculture, Forest Service, Southern Region, Kisatchie National Forest. 83 p.

Kerr, E. 1958. History of forestry in Louisiana. Baton Rouge, LA: Louisiana Forestry Commission. 55 p.

Morgan, E.; Kerr, E. 1962. The Lower Mississippi Valley: a study in photographs and words. Baton Rouge, LA: Claitor's Book Store. [no pagination].

CONCLUSIONS

Virgin pine forests of the South were mostly harvested by the late 1920s. Left in their place were "ghost towns" or towns able to maintain only a feeble existence. Both forest industry and the Forest Service believed that there was no future in southern forestry. In the Clapper Report in 1920, the Forest Service made the statement that "in 15 years the South will become dependent for its own needs upon large importations of lumber from the Pacific Coast" (Heyward 1958). Gifford Pinchot and other conservationists loudly predicted a national timber famine. History had shown that removal of forests resulted in severe conditions such as major soil erosion, change of climate, and droughts that might result in desert conditions.

How did the South avoid the negative results that were predicted from the decimation of its forests? One factor was the resilience of southern pines (MacCleery 2002). If seedlings were established, growth was rapid and new crops helped sustain the ecology of the region.

Another factor was the rapid development of forestry. In about 1900, forestry programs began to be established in universities in the North—those in the South generally came several decades later. Because of the nature of forest conditions in the South, forestry graduates came to address these serious problems. With only a handful of professional foresters, and despite little technical support and primitive working conditions, forestry in the South made tremendous gains. Foresters developed reforestation techniques, studied and began to understand the role of fire in forests, began surveys of the southern forests that led to development and expansion of forest industries, and learned how to control important insect pests and diseases (Barnett 2004).

They also developed an understanding of the importance of the use of statistical design and the value of tree improvement, developed methods for controlling soil erosion, and improved the efficiency of producing forest products.

Within 3 decades, major reforestation efforts were underway and a wide array of forestry

issues was being addressed. After the interruption of World War II, forestry blossomed in the 1950s and 1960s. The success story of southern pine forestry was facilitated by the application of research results generated through cooperative work of the Forest Service, southern forestry schools, State forestry agencies, and forest industry (Fox and others 2007). Productivity was enhanced by contributions of applied silviculture in tree improvement, nursery management, site preparation, weed control, and fertilization to southern pine plantations. The success of pine plantation silviculture has turned the South into the wood basket of the United States

Stands such as this one are common across the South as the result of the practices developed by early foresters. Thanks to the work of these foresters, the South's forests are again the "bread basket of the nation."

(Schultz 1997) and continues to drive the economy of most Southern States. Timber production was an early emphasis, but management of the entire forest ecosystem became an important aspect of the southern forestry enterprise. Southern forestry now represents a means of tying the region to an unfolding age of science with the bonds of soil, climate, and geography that age of King Cotton could never fully forge (Clark 1984). The individuals profiled in this document did much to achieve the success that has been accomplished.

How did our early forestry professionals with limited resources accomplish so much in a relatively short period of time? Dedication, cooperation, and teamwork were characteristics of the early forestry program. Not only did the individuals support each other's efforts, they developed excellent relationships with individuals in universities and other agencies, as well as with those in forest industry and

State organizations dedicated to solving problems common to all organizations. Wakeley (1964) quotes a passage in Macaulay's "Horatius" that describes their attitude:

For Romans in Rome's quarrel
Spared neither goods nor gold
Nor son nor wife nor limb nor life
In the brave days of old.
Then none was for the party.
Then all were for the State.
Then the rich man helped the poor
And the poor man loved the great.
Then lands were fairly portioned.
Then spoils were fairly sold.
The Romans were like brothers
In the brave days of old.

ACKNOWLEDGMENTS

Louisiana Forestry Association's *Forests & People* magazine has been a great source of information on those profiled in the document. Their early 'Faces of Forestry' series did much to provide recognition for those who made major contributions to the development of forestry in the South.

Appreciation is due to Tom Kelly, publisher of the *Piney Woods Journal*, who published a number of these profiles in his magazine which led to the idea of expanding that initiative into this larger project.

LITERATURE CITED

Barnett, J.P. 2004. Southern forest resource conditions and management practices from 1900–1950: benefits of research. In: Gen. Tech. Rep. SRS-75. Asheville, NC: U.S. Department of Agriculture, Forest Service, Southern Research Station: 15-22. Chapter 3.

Boyd, W. 2001. The forests of the future? Industrial forestry and the southern pulp and paper complex. In: Scranton, Philip, ed. The second wave: southern industrialization from the 1940s to the 1970s. Athens, GA: University of Georgia Press: 168-218.

Chapman, H.H. 1912. Forest fires and forestry in the Southern States. American Forestry. 18: 510-517.

Chapman, H.H. 1926. Factors determining natural reproduction of longleaf pine on cutover lands in LaSalle Parish, Louisiana. Bulletin 16. New Haven, CT: Yale University School of Forestry. 44 p

Clark, T.D. 1984. The greening of the South: the recovery of land and forest. Lexington, KY: The University Press of Kentucky. 168 p.

Demmon, E L. 1937. Forests and the economy of the South. Southern Economic Journal. 3(4): 369-380.

Fickle, J.E. 2001. Early forestry in the South and Mississippi. Forest History Today (Spring/Fall): 11-18.

Forbes, R.D. 1923. The passing of the piney woods. American Forests. 29(351): 131-136, 185.

Fox, T.R.; Jokela, E J; Allen, H.L. 2007. The development of pine plantation silviculture in the Southern United States. Journal of Forestry. 105: 337-347.

Heyward, F. 1955. Austin Cary: Yankee peddler in forestry. American Forests. 61(5): 29-30, 43-44; 61(6): 28-29, 52-53.

Heyward, F. 1958. History of industrial forestry in the South. The Colonel William B. Greeley Lectures in industrial forestry. Seattle, WA: University of Washington, College of Forestry. 50 p.

Kerr, Ed. 1958. History of forestry in Louisiana. Baton Rouge, LA: Louisiana Forestry Commission. 55 p.

MacCleery, D.W. 2002. American forests: a history of resiliency and recovery. Durham, NC: Forest History Society. 58 p.

Reed, G. 1982. Saving the naval stores industry: Charles Holmes Herty's cup-and-gutter experiments 1900–1905. Journal of Forest History. 26(4): 168-175.

Reed, G.M. 1995. Realization of a dream: Charles H. Herty and the South's first newsprint mill. Forest & Conservation History. 39: 4-16.

Schultz, R P. 1997. Loblolly pine. The ecology and culture of loblolly pine (*Pinus taeda* L.). Agric. Handb. 713. Washington, DC: U.S. Department of Agriculture, Forest Service. 493 p.

Wahlenberg, W.G. 1960. Loblolly pine. Its use, ecology, regeneration, protection, growth and management. Durham, NC: Duke University. 603 p.

Wakeley, P.C. 1954. Planting the southern pines. Agricultural Monograph 18. Washington, DC: U.S. Department of Agriculture, Forest Service. 233 p.

Wakeley, P.C. 1964. A biased history of the Southern Forest Experiment Station through fiscal year 1933. Unpublished document. New Orleans, LA: On file with: USDA Forest Service, Southern Research Station, Forest Management Research, Pineville, LA 71360.

Wakeley, Philip C. 1976. F.O. (Red) Bateman, pioneer silviculturist. Journal of Forest History. 20(2): 91-99.

Williams, M.1989. Americans and their forests: a historical biography. Cambridge,UK: Cambridge University Press. 599 p.

www.ingramcontent.com/pod-product-compliance
Lightning Source LLC
Chambersburg PA
CBHW081237280526
45787CB00006B/2696